First World War
and Army of Occupation
War Diary
France, Belgium and Germany

61 DIVISION
Divisional Troops
Royal Army Veterinary Corps
61 Mobile Veterinary Section
24 May 1916 - 31 March 1919

WO95/3052/2

The Naval & Military Press Ltd
www.nmarchive.com
Published in association with The National Archives

Published by

The Naval & Military Press Ltd

Unit 10 Ridgewood Industrial Park,

Uckfield, East Sussex,

TN22 5QE England

Tel: +44 (0) 1825 749494

www.naval-military-press.com

www.nmarchive.com

This diary has been reprinted in facsimile from the original. Any imperfections are inevitably reproduced and the quality may fall short of modern type and cartographic standards.

© **Crown Copyright**
Images reproduced by permission of The National Archives, London, England, 2015.

Contents

Document type	Place/Title	Date From	Date To
Heading	WO95/3052/2		
Heading	61st Division 61st Mobile Vety Section May 1916-Mar 1919		
War Diary	Southampton	24/05/1916	25/05/1916
War Diary	Water	25/05/1916	25/05/1916
War Diary	Havre	26/05/1916	27/05/1916
War Diary	St Venant	28/05/1916	12/06/1916
War Diary	La Gorgue	13/06/1916	27/10/1916
War Diary	St Venant	28/10/1916	31/10/1916
War Diary	Beauvoir	12/11/1916	14/11/1916
War Diary	Candas	15/11/1916	15/11/1916
War Diary	Bernevil	16/11/1916	17/11/1916
War Diary	Contay	18/11/1916	21/11/1916
War Diary	Albert	22/11/1916	25/11/1916
War Diary	Martinsart	26/11/1916	16/01/1917
War Diary	Marieux	17/01/1917	17/01/1917
War Diary	Bernaville	18/01/1917	19/01/1917
War Diary	Neuville	20/01/1917	04/02/1917
War Diary	Longpre	05/02/1917	14/02/1917
War Diary	Goeuves	15/02/1917	15/02/1917
War Diary	Aubigny	16/02/1917	16/02/1917
War Diary	Hangard	17/02/1917	19/02/1917
War Diary	Harbonnieres	20/02/1917	28/02/1917
War Diary	Omiecourt	29/03/1917	01/04/1917
War Diary	Billancourt	16/04/1917	21/04/1917
War Diary	Douilly	22/04/1917	30/04/1917
War Diary	Y	01/04/1917	11/04/1917
War Diary	Billancourt	12/04/1917	15/04/1917
War Diary	Douilly	01/05/1917	14/05/1917
War Diary	Bethencourt	15/05/1917	19/05/1917
War Diary	Cayeux	20/05/1917	20/05/1917
War Diary	Glissy	21/05/1917	21/05/1917
War Diary	Naours	22/05/1917	23/05/1917
War Diary	Outre Bois	24/05/1917	07/06/1917
War Diary	L'arbret	08/06/1917	08/06/1917
War Diary	Warlus	09/06/1917	11/06/1917
War Diary	Agnez-Les-Duisans	12/06/1917	21/06/1917
War Diary	Rebreuviette	23/06/1917	23/06/1917
War Diary	Vieil-Hesdin	23/06/1917	24/06/1917
War Diary	Hermel	25/06/1917	26/07/1917
War Diary	Erkelsbrugge	27/07/1917	31/07/1917
War Diary	Poperinghe	15/08/1917	25/08/1917
War Diary	Erkelsbrugge	01/08/1917	14/08/1917
War Diary	Poperinghe	01/09/1917	14/09/1917
War Diary	Watou	15/09/1917	16/09/1917
War Diary	Wormhoudt	17/09/1917	18/09/1917
War Diary	Wanquetin	19/09/1917	19/09/1917
War Diary	Agnez-Lez-Duisans	20/09/1917	24/09/1917
War Diary	Arras G.13.d.8.5	25/09/1917	30/09/1917
War Diary	G.13.d.8.5 Arras-St Pol	01/10/1917	13/10/1917

War Diary	Arras-St Pol	14/10/1917	29/11/1917
War Diary	Beaulencourt	30/11/1917	01/12/1917
War Diary	Etricourt	02/12/1917	23/12/1917
War Diary	Clery	24/12/1917	24/12/1917
War Diary	Etenehem	25/12/1917	30/12/1917
War Diary	Harbonnieres	31/12/1917	06/01/1918
War Diary	Nestle	07/01/1918	10/01/1918
War Diary	Douilly	11/01/1918	21/03/1918
War Diary	Billancourt	22/03/1918	22/03/1918
War Diary	Liancourt Villers-Le-Roye	23/03/1918	23/03/1918
War Diary	Liancourt Damery	24/03/1918	24/03/1918
War Diary	Guyencourt	26/03/1918	27/03/1918
War Diary	Dommartin	28/03/1918	28/03/1918
War Diary	Sains	29/03/1918	30/03/1918
War Diary	Salouel	31/03/1918	06/04/1918
War Diary	Clairy	07/04/1918	07/04/1918
War Diary	Arguel	08/04/1918	12/04/1918
War Diary	Arguel Abbeville	13/04/1918	13/04/1918
War Diary	St Austreberthe	14/04/1918	14/04/1918
War Diary	Petit St Pol (Fruges)	15/04/1918	15/04/1918
War Diary	Lambres	16/04/1918	21/07/1918
War Diary	4.e.5 Wardrecq	22/07/1918	31/07/1918
War Diary	Lambres	01/08/1918	06/08/1918
War Diary	Boeseghem	07/08/1918	01/09/1918
War Diary	Tannay	02/09/1918	04/09/1918
War Diary	Roussel Farm	05/09/1918	03/10/1918
War Diary	Lambres	04/10/1918	05/10/1918
War Diary	Gezaincourt	06/10/1918	07/10/1918
War Diary	Bretoncourt	08/10/1918	08/10/1918
War Diary	St Leger	09/10/1918	09/10/1918
War Diary	Morchies	10/10/1918	10/10/1918
War Diary	Graincourt	11/10/1918	17/10/1918
War Diary	Cambrai	18/10/1918	18/10/1918
War Diary	Rieux	19/10/1918	22/10/1918
War Diary	Avesnes-Lez-Aubert	23/10/1918	25/10/1918
War Diary	Maison-Bleu	26/10/1918	02/11/1918
War Diary	Avesnes-Lez-Aubert	03/11/1918	07/11/1918
War Diary	Bermerain	08/11/1918	13/11/1918
War Diary	Rieux	14/11/1918	14/11/1918
War Diary	Cambrai	15/11/1918	23/11/1918
War Diary	Beugnatre	24/11/1918	24/11/1918
War Diary	St Leger	25/11/1918	25/11/1918
War Diary	Vacquerie	26/11/1918	07/12/1918
War Diary	Oneux	08/12/1918	31/03/1919

130 915/3052/2

61ST DIVISION

61ST MOBILE VETY SECTION

MAY 1916-MAR 1919

61ST DIVISION

WAR DIARY
or
INTELLIGENCE SUMMARY.
(Erase heading not required.)

Army Form C. 2118.

Vol 1 — 61 of Mob. Vet. Sec.

Place	Date	Hour	Summary of Events and Information	Remarks and references to Appendices
Southampton	24.5.16	7.30 pm	Left Amesbury at 2.15 pm. 1 officer, 26 men including 3 a.s.c. attached, 2 Lembros wagons & 1 Supply G.S. Wagon. Arrived S'hampton 4 pm. One horse casualty. Horse exchanged. Embarked on S.S. Rosetti with 30 r 2 Bde R.F.A. Left S'hampton 6 pm.	R.J. Livingstone O.C.

Army Form C. 2118.

WAR DIARY
or
INTELLIGENCE SUMMARY.
(Erase heading not required.)

Instructions regarding War Diaries and Intelligence Summaries are contained in F. S. Regs., Part II. and the Staff Manual respectively. Title pages will be prepared in manuscript.

61st d. No. Mob Vet Sec.

Place	Date	Hour	Summary of Events and Information	Remarks and references to Appendices
Shrapston Cates	25.5.16	7.30 pm	Checked in Shrapston Gates from 6pm 24.5.16 to 6pm 25.6.16. 6pm started for Havre.	E.J. Lewis
Havre	26.5.16	7.30 pm	Arrived Havre 6am. Disembarked 9.15am without casualty. 10.30am Proceeded to No 1 Rest Camp with guide. Put up horse lines & 3 tents for men. 1/o O.C. E.J. Lewis
	27.5.16	5pm	O/C gam proceeded to A/C station. Left horse lines. No.1 injured. E.J. Lewis
			Struck camp 5pm.
St Venant	28.5.16	10pm	Entrained Havre with 26 men 1 interpreter 1 officer, 26 horses. 3.45pm. at 4.30pm. Left Havre 9.30pm. Proceeded to Rouen, Boulogne, Abbeville. Arrived Chocques 3pm. Detrained without casualty. 5pm Proceeded to La Haye, St Venant, arriving at 9pm. Put up horse lines. E.J. Lewis
do	29.5.16	10pm	Cleaned up Farm. 1 Shoegh Rgt. 2/5 th Gloucester Rgt.	E.J. Lewis
do	30.5.16	10pm	Rct from 2/5 Gloucester Rgt Shoegh.	E.J. Lewis
do	31.5.16	10pm	1 Horse from D.C.L.D. Suffolk reg. Visit Abs 1 & 2 Coy D.A.C.	E.J. Lewis
do	1.6.16	10pm	Visit D.A.C. 5 horses + mule hospl in. Most & Coy. Sistern. 1 horse hosp in . Nos	E.J. Lewis Capt O.C.
			Shoegh. No. 1 Coy. Cracked heel abot.	

T2134. Wt. W708-776. 500000. 4/15. Sir J. C. & S.

WAR DIARY or INTELLIGENCE SUMMARY

Army Form C. 2118.

June 1916 Vol II

61st Mobile Vet Sec

Place	Date	Hour	Summary of Events and Information	Remarks and references to Appendices
St Vineant	1-6-16	10pm	9am Visit DAC 5 horses + mules brought in to Section. Visit No 3 174 Coy Divl Train Horse thought in. 1 case strangles Off 1 Coy ASC Cracked Heels Ltd	E.J. Lewis
St Venant	2-6-16	10pm	9am Visit all horses in 61st DAC. 1pm Section. 3.30pm ADVS conference.	E.J. Lewis
"	3-6-16	do	9am Visit all horses in 11th DAC. Billeting forms re afternoon Section. 1 case suspected Mange	E.J. Lewis
"	4-6-16	do	Church parade. Inspect rifles + accoutrements of men. Visit 61st DAC. Visit from ADVS	E.J. Lewis
"	5-6-16	do	Visit all horses of D.A.C. 2pm Section. Inspect Saddles.	E.J. Lewis
"	6-6-16	do	Visit all horses of D.A.C. 2pm Section. Inspect rifles + rifle drill	E.J. Lewis
"	7-6-16	do	Visit all horses of D.A.C. 2pm Section. Physical exercise	E.J. Lewis
"	8-6-16	do	Visit all horses of D.A.C. 2pm Section. 3.30pm ADVS Conference.	E.J. Lewis
"	9-6-16	do	Visit all horses of D.A.C. 2pm Section. Inspect rifles rifle drill.	E.J. Lewis
"	10-6-16	do	Visit all horses of D.A.C. 2pm Section. Physical drill	E.J. Lewis
"	11-6-16	do	Visit all horses of D.A.C. 2pm Section. Inspect rifles	E.J. Lewis
"	12-6-16	do	Visit Standings + billets of 3rd Coll V. Sect La Gorgue. Evacuated 12 horses from Merville. 2pm Section	E.J. Lewis
La Gorgue	13-6-16	do	8am Strike camp with Section reproceed to La Gorgue. Take over Farm with 3 horses standings + billets for men, 1 room in cnt of 3 horses + 1 left.	E.J. Lewis
"	14-6-16	do	Visit No 1 + 2 Sections DAC. 1st Batch Required. US re a Merville Rd 2 to Section	E.J. Lewis O.C.

WAR DIARY
or
INTELLIGENCE SUMMARY.
(Erase heading not required.)

Army Form C. 2118.

Summary of Events and Information: Visit J.M. Mobile Vet Sec.

Place	Date	Hour	Summary of Events and Information	Remarks and references to Appendices
La Bassée	15.11.15	10 p	Visit all lines of D.A.C, 2 pr Section. Inspect rifles. Evening men Inspect billets. Sent for horse feed.	E.J. Laird
do	16.11.15	10 p	Visit D.A.C. 2 pr Section. Repair hock stitching for horse. 3.30 A.D.V.S Conference.	E.J. Laird
do	17.11.15	10 p	Visit D.A.C. horse. 2 pr Section. Repair stitching. Inspect rifles saddles.	E.J. Laird
do	18.11.15	10 p	Visit D.A.C. Evacuate 11 horses by rail to Neufchatel. Clean up Section farm	E.J. Laird
do	19.11.15	10 p	Visit D.A.C. 2 pr Section. Repairs to harness.	E.J. Laird
do	20.11.15	10 p	Visit D.A.C. 2 pr Section.	E.J. Laird
do	21.11.15	10 p	Visit D.A.C. 2 pr Section. Inspect rifles.	E.J. Laird
do	22.11.15	10 p	Visit D.A.C. 2 pr Section.	E.J. Laird
do	23.11.15	10 p	Visit D.A.C. 3.30 pm A.D.V.S. Conference. Receive float from Abbeville.	E.J. Laird
do	24.11.15	10 p	Visit D.A.C. 2 pr Section. Inspect rifles. Particulars of horses for evacuation	E.J. Laird
do	25.11.15	10 p	Visit D.A.C. 2 pr Section. Evacuate 26 horses by rail to Neufchatel	E.J. Laird
do	26.11.15	10 p	Visit D.A.C. 2 pr Section. Inspect rifles + saddles	E.J. Laird
do	27.11.15	10 p	Visit D.A.C. 2 pr Section. Particulars of horses marks for evacuation	E.J. Laird
do	28.11.15	10 p	Visit D.A.C. 2 pr Section. Evacuate 16 horses + mules to Neufchatel.	E.J. Laird
do	29.11.15	10 p	Visit D.A.C. 2 pr Section. Inspect rifles.	E.J. Laird
do	30.11.15	10 p	Visit D.A.C. 2 pr Section. Inspect saddles + kit	E.J. Laird
				O.C. Capt

WAR DIARY or INTELLIGENCE SUMMARY

Army Form C. 2118.

Vol III

61 Mot Vet Section

Place	Date	Hour	Summary of Events and Information	Remarks and references to Appendices
La Gorgue	13/1/16	10pm	9am Lake marks no. of horses for evacuation & write out Evacuation returns. 11.30am Visit Glamorgan by R.R. in Estaires. Bad condition. 1pm tea & 2 horses to base. 1 shoeing? Inefficient. 2pm C.O./Sect D.A.C. Visit condition inferior a little. 6pm went to Reserve Park A.S.C. 7.30pm visit Col. 1 Coy A.S.C. & at horse. Ruptures stained. Sonem Col. Stevenson re getting no food in S.I. Large quantity of food from stores in Postal cavity.	
do	14/1/16	10pm	9am. Visit Nos 3,4 & 1 Section. Shoeing mules over grown hoofs stopped owing to numerous cases. 2pm. attends? horses for evacuation. Weekly return. 3.30pm. Visit A.D.V.S. for weekly meeting. Spend evening at section.	
do	15/1/16	10pm	9am went to meals & animals & 2 horses by train from Estaires. 10pm Visit No 1 Section D.A.C. at La Gorgue - affirmation with section. No 1 Sect D A C Removed to Ebenville R.I.	
do	16/1/16	10pm	9am Visit Nos 1, 3 & 4 Section DAC. Also No 1 Petrol Park RR. 11am No 2 Section DAC. afternoon & evening with Section.	

WAR DIARY
or
INTELLIGENCE SUMMARY.
(Erase heading not required.)

Army Form C. 2118.

Instructions regarding War Diaries and Intelligence Summaries are contained in F. S. Regs., Part II. and the Staff Manual respectively. Title pages will be prepared in manuscript.

Place	Date	Hour	Summary of Events and Information	Remarks and references to Appendices
La Gorgue	9.7.16	10pm	Inspect sick & sand cases of No 1 Sect. 6th D.A.C. at 10 am. Visit by A.D.V.S. evening. Inspect all cars for Cadre Col. Kearn. 1 A.S.C. man reported sickness. Section afternoon.	
La Gorgue	10.7.16	10pm	Proceed 8 animals to Steam ambulance in hope of extricate. 7.30am in charge of S/Sadler & three men. Inspect shoes & nails of 1 Sect. 1st Pontoon Park R.E. No 3. 4 + 2 Section 61st D.A.C. Bring in fresh cases of S/Sergn 1st Army L.R.E. 61st Section in afternoon.	
La Gorgue	11.7.16	10pm	Inspect animals of No 1 Sect 1st D.A.C. at La Force. Collection parade. any heavy work. Remove rounds for details. Collect one animal from same unit with strained knots in float. Section afternoon. L. Caslon. Visit by General MacKenzie & A.S.E.	
La Gorgue	12.7.16	10pm	9am Visit 1 Sect Pontoon Park R.E. No 3. 4 + 2 Section D.A.C. 2 of 2 Section find one case of injury. Afternoon at Lection. Rearrange Bridge. Visit by A.D.V.S. for evacuations. Rifle inspection (food). Pay Parade.	

T2134. Wt. W708—776. 500000. 4/15. Sir J. C. & B.

WAR DIARY or INTELLIGENCE SUMMARY

Army Form C. 2118.

Place	Date	Hour	Summary of Events and Information	Remarks and references to Appendices
La Boyne	17/7/16	10 pm	Examine all cases of Nos 3 & 4 Sections. D.A.C. Condition poor. Remain with Section all afternoon.	
d°	18/7/16	10 pm	9am Shelling (intermitent) 108 horses make up. No/Sect D.A.C. Visit Nos 3, 4 & 5 Sections. Examine cases at Palace Station. Light shock. A.D.V.S. Examine horses for evacuation 6pm. Jn/Hy Section funds.	
d°	19/7/16	10 pm	9am Examine horses with No 10/16 Evacuation. Sent 174 horses make up & sent D.A.C. Visit Bichetin. Take description of horses in Section for evacuation. La Boyne held.	
d°	27/7/16	10 pm	Nos 1 make up 210 horses make up at No 6 section D.M.C. dispatches preparations preparation at A.D.V.S. duties.	
d°	28/7/16	10 pm	Examine horses make evacuated at ol & 2 Sect A.D.V.S. meeting J. Officers.	
d°	29/7/16	10 pm	9am Le horses make of No 1, 8, 4, 7 44pm D.A.C. Section afternoon	
d°	30/7/16	10 pm	Section A.D.V.S. twice. Examine animals for evacuation. Divis at General's.	
d°	31/7/16	10 pm	Sent 202 horses make at cl° 3 Sect D.A.C. 112 90 hits Evacuation for A.D.V.S visit	

WAR DIARY or INTELLIGENCE SUMMARY

Army Form C. 2118.

Mob Vty Sec Vol 4

Place	Date	Hour	Summary of Events and Information	Remarks and references to Appendices
La Gorgue	1/7/16	10pm	5am Evacuate 26 horses + mules (casualties) to base by trps from Etaires Corps H.Qrs + Bundle.	E.J. Lewis
			9am Visit Nos 1, 2, 3, 4 + 2 Sections DAC. Everything satisfactory. 2 pm all lines for horses	E.J. Lewis
			in Section. Sent 3 horses to Base Dep by rail (Pte Brock)	E.J. Lewis
do	2/7	10pm	8.30. Int (intestinally) 9 horses + 29 mules of Headquarters 6" DAC. All good. Visit Nos	E.J. Lewis
			3 R Sections DAC. 9 pm Mobile Subn.	
do	3/7/16	10pm	8.30. Visit H.Qrs DAC + Nos 12. 3 O+ Sections + Relais Park R.E. Afternoon at stables.	E.J. Lewis
	4/7/16	10pm	Seconds Inspect Rifles Men + Horse Wile 9. Mr HQ horses. Sympaten.	E.J. Lewis
	5/7/16	10pm	Visit No 3 7+ Section DAC. Section - ADVS Conference	E.J. Lewis
	6/7/16	10pm	Visit all DAC. Remove horses from stable, air all stables. All on parade in muster sheets for Sheyfel.	E.J. Lewis
	7/7/16	10pm	Visit 2 DAC + check O.C. with parasites of lads under examin.	E.J. Lewis
	8/7/16	10pm	Visit Nos 1 - 3 - 4 DAC. 1 Pte Lyff Bat these horses, Perform for evacuation.	E.J. Lewis
	9/7/16	10pm	Evacuate 22 horses + mules to base by trps. Visit DAC (all) with A/S	E.J. Lewis
	10/7/16	10pm	Visit Nos 1 - 3 - 4 Sections DAC. 2 pm Section Inspect men rifles + kits.	E.J. Lewis
	11/7/16	10pm	Visit all 2 Coy HAC. 2 pm Section.	E.J. Lewis
	12/7/16	10pm	Visit all Nos 1 - 3 - 4 Sections DAC. Visit for General. 2.30 ADVS Conference	E.J. Lewis
			Visit all 2 Coy DAC. 2 pm Section. Examine all animals.	E.J. Lewis

WAR DIARY
or
INTELLIGENCE SUMMARY.
(Erase heading not required.)

Army Form C. 2118.

Place	Date	Hour	Summary of Events and Information	Remarks and references to Appendices
La Gorgue	13/2/16	10 pm	Section. Prepare all horse rounds & like particulars for transition. Inspection by ADVS. Visit by General Matthews & SA 2 & 6. Prepare lists of animals earmarked for Hd 6 1st Division. Rifle inspection. Kit by transit of Horses	E J Lane
do	14/2/16	10 pm	9 am Visit ets 1 - 3 - 4 Sections DAC. Special attention to feeding. Section late. all animals for evacuation tpd properly. General called. April 2 horses Metcalfe.	E J Lane
do	15/2/16	10 pm	8 am. Sent 20 horses mules on loan at Estaires for St Omer. 9.30 am Visit ADVS. 10 am Sent 21 horses from La Gorgue station to Boulogne by train. 11 am Visit ets 2 Section. DAC. 2 pm Section. Sic horses.	E J Lane
do	16/2/16	10 pm	9 am Visit ets 1 - 3 - 4 Section DAC. 2 pm Section. Receive 10 loads of hooks for standings. Rifle inspection.	E J Lane
do	17/2/16	10 pm	Visit ets 2 Section DAC. ADVS visited Section. Prepare for evacuation of horses.	E J Lane
do	18/2/16	10 pm	Visit ets 1 - 3 & 4 Sections. DAC. 2 pm Remove sick & fat from lines with farriers transit of Horses. 8.30 pm ADVS. Receive 5 loads of broken mules for standings. Rifle inspection.	E J Lane
do	19/2/16	10 pm	Sell carcase & hides for frs 200. Visit ets 2 Section DAC. Start loading horse standings. Receive instructions re the transit of horses & bread and ammo.	E J Lane

WAR DIARY or INTELLIGENCE SUMMARY

Army Form C. 2118.

(Erase heading not required.)

Place	Date	Hour	Summary of Events and Information	Remarks and references to Appendices
La Boyne	20th June	10 pm	9 am Visit to Pos 1-3 & 4 sections D.A.C. See about handing all horses and what's over when brand is not returnable (large percentage) Visit by ADVS to arrange amounts the evacuated. Continue with standing patrons.	S.J. Lewis
do	21st	10 pm	9 am Sent internally 131 mules & 23 horses of 6 & 4 Sections D.A.C. Section in afternoon report of casualties. Prepare for evacuation of horses.	S.J. Lewis
do	22nd	10 pm	7.45 am Sent 12 horses & mules & heavy type from Padua Service Party 10th C.C. Ross for hospital. Visit all amounts in the DAC & review those rejected yesterday. Reexamine Section also No 3-2-1 Sections DAC invalid.	S.J. Lewis
do	23rd	10 pm	8 am Visit Nos 1-3-4 Section DAC. Section in afternoon visit from ADVS. Prepare for evacuation. Say men receive two remounts told leave.	D.J. Lewis
do	24th	10 pm	8 am Visit Nos 2 Section DAC. Afternoon with State Branch & arrival by lyceh line.	S.J. Lewis
do	25th	10 pm	8 am Visit Nos 1-3 & 4 Sections DAC. 3.30 pm ADVS meeting.	S.J. Lewis
do	26th	10 pm	8 am No 2 Section DAC. ADVS visit section. Buck starting enterics.	S.J. Lewis
do	27th	10 pm	Section all day. 7.15 pm Col. Witcomb Vetnary mule will fractured ulna. Visit by ADVS.	S.J. Lewis
do	28th	10 pm	Visit CBC 1-3-4 Section DAC. Examines for evacuation. Standing. Visit 10 Canadian CCS	S.J. Lewis
do	29th	1 pm	Sent 114 horses & mules to hosp (thro) 2 horses to Boulogne (mange). Visit No 2 Sect DAC. Continue standing ec.	D.J. Lewis

Army Form C. 2118.

WAR DIARY
or
INTELLIGENCE SUMMARY.
(Erase heading not required.)

Instructions regarding War Diaries and Intelligence Summaries are contained in F. S. Regs., Part II. and the Staff Manual respectively. Title pages will be prepared in manuscript.

Place	Date	Hour	Summary of Events and Information	Remarks and references to Appendices
La Gorgue	30/6	10pm	8 am Visit OPs 1 - 3 - 4 Section 99C. Shot at all day. Artillery brisk 2/L Sch. F.A. Slack 9 & 10. Shrases from Metecten DAK. Prepare for manoeuvres.	S/Lieut
do	2/7	10pm	Sent 2 horses + 2 mules to 8 bau by barge. Became the 2 Oct DAK Section Bench Range S/L Laus	S/L Laus

Army Form C. 2118.

WAR DIARY
or
INTELLIGENCE SUMMARY.

(Erase heading not required.)

Instructions regarding War Diaries and Intelligence Summaries are contained in F. S. Regs., Part II. and the Staff Manual respectively. Title pages will be prepared in manuscript.

Place	Date	Hour	Summary of Events and Information	Remarks and references to Appendices

T/2134. Wt. W708—776. 500000. 4/15. Sir J. C. & S.

Army Form C. 2118.

WAR DIARY
or
INTELLIGENCE SUMMARY.
(Erase heading not required.)

Vol 5

Instructions regarding War Diaries and Intelligence Summaries are contained in F.S. Regs., Part II. and the Staff Manual respectively. Title pages will be prepared in manuscript.

Place	Date	Hour	Summary of Events and Information	Remarks and references to Appendices
La Gorge	1-9-16	10 pm	Section all day. Treats all cases in & continue with standings other than oral troubles	E.J. Lewis.
do	2-9-16	10 pm	Horse shoes all day. Section is weary sore traces.	E.J. Lewis.
do	3-9-16	10 pm	Men examine all horse in D.A.C. & cases of pricked up nails or punched feet	E.J. Lewis.
do	4-9-16	10 pm	8 am Visit Nos 1-3-4 Section D.A.C. & 1st Donton Park R.E. Prepare for Evacuation Rifle Inspection	E.J. Lewis.
do	5-9-16	10 pm	8 am Visit Nb 2 Section D.A.C. Visit Nb 1 Section D.A.C. with A.D.V.S. Evacuate 10 horse mules	E.J. Lewis.
do	6-9-16	10 pm	8 am Visit Nos 1-3-4 Sections D.A.C. Evacuate 1 horse to Boulogne with Mange. Continue standing w. at Section.	E.J. Lewis.
do	7-9-16	10 pm	Visit Nb 2 Section D.A.C. Dark horse with Lamphet Gtd. Section afternoon. Evacuate 8 horse	E.J. Lewis.
do	8-9-16	10 pm	Visit A.D.V.S. re evacuations. Visit Nos 1 - 3 - 4 Sections D.A.C. & 1st Donton Park R.E. A.D.V.S. meeting afternoon.	E.J. Lewis.
do	9-9-16	10 pm	Visit Nb 2 Section D.A.C. Section afternoon. Full marching order parade.	E.J. Lewis.
do	10-9-16	10 pm	Section all day. Improvements to standings &c. Prepare for evacuation	E.J. Lewis.
do	11-9-16	10 pm	Car to Calais re visit Nb 4 Base Vety Hospital	E.J. Lewis.
do	12-9-16	10 pm	Visit Nb 1- 3- 4 Sections D.A.C. morning Nb 2 Section D.A.C. afternoon. Section Evening	E.J. Lewis.
do			Send 4 animals to St Omer by barge	E.J. Lewis.
do	13-9-16	10 pm	Visit Nos 2 - 3 - 4 Section D.A.C. Section afternoon. See all cases	E.J. Lewis.

Army Form C. 2118.

WAR DIARY
or
INTELLIGENCE SUMMARY.
(Erase heading not required.)

Instructions regarding War Diaries and Intelligence Summaries are contained in F.S. Regs., Part II. and the Staff Manual respectively. Title page will be prepared in manuscript.

Place	Date	Hour	Summary of Events and Information	Remarks and references to Appendices
La Lipre	14/2/16	10pm	Visit 1st Bastion Pack R.E. & No. 2 Section D.A.C. Section decomp. camp. 7.15 pm visit by General Wilkinson	E.J. Lewis
do	15/2/16	9pm	Visit C.B. 1. 9 & 4 Section D.A.C. Horse destroyed. 1st Battion Section. Visit A.D.V.S. weekly return	E.J. Lewis
do	16/2/16	10pm	Visit No. 2 Section DAC. A.D.V.S. Visit Section. Capt. Pool sent to Cassel in Section work	E.J. Lewis
do	17/2/16	10pm	Visit A. 3 Section A.D.C. & various items for horse transferred. Duty Camp Veterinary attention	E.J. Lewis
do			S.d party for 12 horses. 1 shot of road.	E.J. Lewis
do	18/2/16	10pm	Gen Visit CBs 1. 3. & 4 Section DAC also 1st Battion Pack RE Visit from A.D.V.S. Section Report & evacuation	E.J. Lewis
do	19/2/16	10pm	Gen Visit CB 2 Section D.A.C. Evacuate 1 mule. 1 horse & 1 horse by large. Afternoon attention. Sick cases or Special attention to Cardin Lewis cases.	E.J. Lewis
do	20/2/16	10pm	Gen Visit CBs 3 - 4 Section D.A.C. No Evacuations. No speram to Boulogne by Van Capt. Pittard & two. ambulance Staff camp. Visit ADVS. Afternoon Rifle infected. 915 pay-parade. 2.37 Col. Lake convoy 9 for horse started up to what for internal	E.J. Lewis
do	21/2/16	10pm	Visit CB. 2 Section. DAC. Afternoon Sick attended. Several cases.	E.J. Lewis
do	22/2/16	10pm	Visit CB 3 & 4 Section DAC. Afternoon Section H. 3.30. Several cases. 8.30 POWS on form 6.15 pm. R ell to hosp for Freud Strong (Cook) S.and Seyt S. Poole & Smith Horse Continue with improvements & good	E.J. Lewis

Army Form C. 2118.

WAR DIARY
or
INTELLIGENCE SUMMARY.
(Erase heading not required.)

Instructions regarding War Diaries and Intelligence Summaries are contained in F. S. Regs., Part II. and the Staff Manual respectively. Title pages will be prepared in manuscript.

Place	Date	Hour	Summary of Events and Information	Remarks and references to Appendices
La Gorgue	23/9/16	10pm	Visit to Nos 2-3-4 Section DAC. Afternoon athletics. General case in.	E.J. Laine
"	24/9/16	10pm	Morning at Section. Overall seen & continue improvements. 6pm of 2 Section DAC with ADVS re-ouylis horses of the Artillery	E.J. Laine
"	25/9/16	10pm	Gen. Visit of No 3 & 4 Section DAC. 26 Animals Evacuated into Section. Examine all animals & take numbers for evacuation. Visit by A.D.V.S. Examining all horses for evacuation.	E.J. Laine
"	26/9/16	10am	Evacuate 19 horses + 1 mule at 8 am & 7.30 am. Visit of No 2 Section DAC. Examine all horses in Section & 1st Pioneers	E.J. Laine
"	27/9/16	10pm	Visit of No 3 re Section DAC. Evacuate 26 Veterinary + 2 Remount cases at Berguette by train. Afternoon at Section. Gd hypertr Sebe	E.J. Laine
"	28/9/16	10pm	Visit of No 2 Section DAC. Afternoon Section. Examine Officers unofficial Startups	E.J. Laine
"	29/9/16	10am	Visit No 3 - 4 Section DAC. Cases at Section. Draw timber for upright & Shedings from C.R.E. ADVS conference.	E.J. Laine
"	30/9/16	10pm	Visit Nos 2-3-4 Sections DAC. Afternoon at Section. Continue improvements. Men see trains.	E.J. Laine

T2134. Wt. W708-776. 500000. 4/15. Sir J. C. & S.

Army Form C. 2118.

WAR DIARY
or
INTELLIGENCE SUMMARY.
(Erase heading not required.)

Instructions regarding War Diaries and Intelligence Summaries are contained in F.S. Regs., Part II. and the Staff Manual respectively. Title pages will be prepared in manuscript.

2/1st S.M. MOBILE VETERINARY SECTION
No.
Date
51st DIVISION

Place	Date	Hour	Summary of Events and Information	Remarks and references to Appendices
La Gorgue	1/10/16	10pm	Section all day dress all cases. 12 noon visit from ADVS to examine horses for evacuation.	E. J. Laws
		4.30pm	Visit from ADVMS & ADVS reference standing for horse Rifle inspection.	E. J. Laws
do	2/10/16	10pm	Visit No 3rd Section DAC. See all horses Section Visit from General McKenzie & Brigadier Col Duffus Brown ADVS in particular	E. J. Laws
do	3/10/16	10pm	Evacuated Horses 2 mules by truck & 8 horses Visit Glasgow R.B. & r.B. 2 Section D.T.T. afternoon.	
			Section. Evening Colic cases at 6th Reserve Park & Glasgow R.B.'s.	E. J. Laws
do	4/10/16	10pm	Visit Glasgow R.B.'s & obs 3rd Section D.T.T. Section Inspect Rifle.	E. J. Laws
do	5/10/16	10pm	Visit obs 2 Section D.A.C. Section 2 men later ill with Influenza.	E. J. Laws
do	6/10/16	10pm	Visit obs 3rd Section D.A.C. Section Sergt Bewel ill Influenza.	E. J. Laws
do	7/10/16	10pm	Visit obs 2 Section D.T.T. Self & 4 men Influenza.	E. J. Laws
do	8/10/16	10pm	4 more men Influenza.	E. J. Laws
do	9/10/16	10pm	2 more men Influenza. Visit by twenty DAVS reminder of horses for evacuation. Report Rifle. Visit obs 3rd Section D.A.C.	E. J. Laws
do	10/10/16	10pm	Visit No 2 Section D.A.C. Send 9 horses & 3 mules to S. C. brew by Barge. Section all afternoon.	E. J. Laws
do	11/10/16	10pm	9am Visit obs 3 & 4 Sections D.A.C. See to all cases in hospital. 1 Dr C.a. & 1 pte returned to duty. 2 privates admitted to hospital.	E. J. Laws

Army Form C. 2118.

WAR DIARY
or
INTELLIGENCE SUMMARY.
(Erase heading not required.)

Instructions regarding War Diaries and Intelligence Summaries are contained in F. S. Regs., Part II. and the Staff Manual respectively. Title pages will be prepared in manuscript.

Place	Date	Hour	Summary of Events and Information	Remarks and references to Appendices
Le Cateau & environs	12/10	10pm	Visit ob 2 Section DAC. Roof fling with Section. Evening ob 3 Section DAC. Three mules with taken sick. Lett of saddle horse of Driver shotly by order of ADVS.	S.J. Lanc
do	13/10	10pm	Visit ob 3 & 4 Section DAC. Section forming all animals in farm.	S.J. Lanc
do	14/10	10pm	Visit Sham Army hospital by R.E. & ob 2 Section DAC. Section	S.J. Lanc
do	15/10	10pm	Section prepare for inoculation. Inspection of men's kits & rifles	S.J. Lanc
do	16/10	10pm	Visit ob 3 & 4 Section DAC. Inspection by ADVS. Section	S.J. Lanc
do	17/10	10pm	Evacuate 27 horses & mules by hospital train. Visit ob 2 Section DAC. Section afternoon.	S.J. Lanc
do	18/10	10pm	Visit ob 3 & 4 Section DAC. & ob 1 Cy 11 Division Train. Section afternoon	S.J. Lanc
do	19/10	10pm	Visit ob 2 Section DAC. Section afternoon	S.J. Lanc
do	20/10	10pm	Visit ob 3 & 4 Section DAC. 1st Remount Park R.E. & ob 1 Cy ASC. Section 8.30 Visit. ADVS with returns.	S.J. Lanc
do	21/10	10pm	Visit ob 2 Section DAC. Section afternoon.	S.J. Lanc
do	22/10	10/a	Visit ob 1 Cy ASC. Section rest of day.	S.J. Lanc
do	23/10	10pm	Visit ob 3 & 4 Section DAC & ob 1 Cy ASC. Visit by ADVS. Three horses for evacuation. Prepare for evacuation	S.J. Lanc

Army Form C. 2118.

WAR DIARY
or
INTELLIGENCE SUMMARY.
(Erase heading not required.)

Instructions regarding War Diaries and Intelligence Summaries are contained in F.S. Regs., Part II. and the Staff Manual respectively. Title pages will be prepared in manuscript.

Stamp: S.M. MOBILE VETERINARY SECTION, 51st DIVISION

Place	Date	Hour	Summary of Events and Information	Remarks and references to Appendices
La Gorgue	24/10/16	10am	Visit 2/3 & 2 led DAC & 1 Coy A.S.C. H/qr Erquinghem 2 horses 12 miles by hyke & steam.	E.J. Lewis
do	25/10/16	10am	Visit HQ 3rd Echelon DAC. Section.	E.J. Lewis
do	26/10/16	10am	Visit CPO & Sect DAC. Section. Visit by A.D.V.S. Visit by returning C.O. a.M.V.S.	E.J. Lewis
do	27/10/16	1pm	Section. Prepare for move. Erquinghem 11 horses + 2 mules. Car to St Venant school.	E.J. Lewis
			Attk. Begin standing up.	
St Venant	28/10/16	1pm	Pack up all kits. Started over to incoming Section. Stables Camp 11am + proceed to St Venant. Take up billets + put up horse lines in. Report to A.D.V.S. dismounted troops	E.J. Lewis
St Venant	29/10/16	10am	Exercise horses. Continue clipping. Saddle rifle cleaning.	E.J. Lewis
do	30/10/16	10am	Exercise horses. Clipping. Extra men evening. Visit from A.D.V.S.	E.J. Lewis
do	31/10/16	10am	do Visit from A.D.V.S. 2 cases lymph.	E.J. Lewis

WAR DIARY
or
INTELLIGENCE SUMMARY.
(Erase heading not required.)

Army Form C. 2118.

Place	Date	Hour	Summary of Events and Information	Remarks and references to Appendices
Beauval	12/7/16		Took over command of M.V.S. Evacuated 9 horses & 2 mules to A.V.Corps	Ack Recd
	13/7/16		Collected one horse from Div. Cn. A.S.C. at DEECHES. Chy - one horse	Ack Recd
	14/7/16		Collected 2 horses from Reserve Rly pains & 60 (?) R.F.A.	Ack Recd
Candas	15/7/16	8.30 am	Left Beauval Arrived Candas 4 pm. Evac 2 hors troters & Bur.	Ack Recd
Beauval	16/7/16	8.40 am	Left Candas Arr Beauval 11.30 am Billeting	Ack Recd
	17/7/16		Collected one Officers horse from 8/4 Coy R.S.C. at DEECHES	Ack Recd
Contay	18/7/16	9.30 am	Left Beauval Arrived Contay 4.30 pm	Ack Recd
	19/7/16		Collected 2 horses from WARLOY belonging to 6th Cheshire Regt. Collected 1 from VADENCOURT belonging to 2.2 MVS	Ack Recd
	20/7/16		Attending to horses in Section & arranging Evacuation	Ack Recd
	21/7/16		Evacuated 15 horses & 1 mule from BRIE EGLISE	Ack Recd
Albert	22/7/16		Left CONTAY 10.45 am arrived ALBERT 2.15 pm took over lines from 30 D.V.S. 30 m V.S. & 4 horses & 1 mule	Ack Recd
	23/7/16		3 O.V.C men arrived of duty from 30 D V.S.	Ack Recd
	24/7/16		Evacuated 15 horses & 1 mule to FORGES LES EAUX	Ack Recd
	25/7/16		Attended to work of Section in camp	Ack Recd
Anderscad	26/7/16		Left ALBERT 10 am arrived at MARTINSART 12.30. Evacuated 7 horses & 1 mule	Ack Recd
	27/7/16		Received horses No. 182 attached D.R.S.	Ack Recd

T2134. Wt. W708—776. 500000. 4/15. Sir J. C. & S.

WAR DIARY
or
INTELLIGENCE SUMMARY.

(Erase heading not required.)

Army Form C. 2118.

Place	Date	Hour	Summary of Events and Information	Remarks and references to Appendices
Marimont	28/11		Attended to work of Section	at Rest
"	29/11		Evacuated 16 horses to FORGES LES EAUX	at Rest
"	30/11		Attended to work of Section	at Rest

Army Form C. 2118.

WAR DIARY
or
INTELLIGENCE SUMMARY.
(Erase heading not required.)

Instructions regarding War Diaries and Intelligence Summaries are contained in F. S. Regs., Part II. and the Staff Manual respectively. Title pages will be prepared in manuscript.

Vol 8

Place	Date	Hour	Summary of Events and Information	Remarks and references to Appendices
Mardinant	17/12		Attended to work of Section. Cnf Sergt & 5 men returned to No 1 Hospital	AV Rept
	18/12		Attended to work of Section	AV Rept
	19/12		Evacuated 10 horses & 1 mule. 8 Horses & 1 Mule belonging to 61 Divn	AV Rept
	20/12		Evacuated 22 horses	AV Rept
	21/12		Attended to work of Section	AV Rept
	22/12		Evacuated 10 horses & 2 mules. 5 Horses & 1 Mule belonging to 61 Divn	AV Rept
	23/12		Attended to work of Section	AV Rept
	24/12		Attended to work of Section	AV Rept
	25/12		Attended to work of Section	AV Rept
	26/12		Evacuated 30 horses & 2 mules. 18 Horses & 2 mules belonging to 61 Divn	AV Rept
	27/12		Attended to work of Section	AV Rept
	28/12		Attended to work of Section	AV Rept
	29/12		Evacuated 26 horses & 6 mules. 26 Horses belonging to 61 Divn	AV Rept
	30/12		Attended to work of Section	AV Rept
	31/12		Evacuated 31 horses & 6 mules. 30 Horses & 6 mules belonging to 61 Divn	AV Rept

T2134. Wt. W708—776. 500000. 4/15. Sir J. C. & S.

Army Form C. 2118.

WAR DIARY
or
INTELLIGENCE SUMMARY.
(Erase heading not required.)

Instructions regarding War Diaries and Intelligence Summaries are contained in F. S. Regs., Part II. and the Staff Manual respectively. Title pages will be prepared in manuscript.

Place	Date	Hour	Summary of Events and Information	Remarks and references to Appendices
Mashonaland	1/2/16		Evacuated 21 horses & 1 mule - 16 horses & 1 mule belonging to 61st Div	Rest Recd
"	2/2/16		Attending to work of section in Camp	Ans Recd
	3/2/16		Evacuated 22 horses & 2 mules	Ans Recd
	4/2/16		Attend to work of section in Camp	Ans Recd
	5/2/16		Evacuated 18 horses & 6 mules. 7 horses & 1 mule belonging to 61st Div	Ans Recd
	6/2/16		Attending to work of section	Ans Recd
	7/2/16		Evacuated 13 horses & 6 mules. 8 horses & 6 mules belonging to 61st Div	Ans Recd
	8/2/16		Attended to work of section	Ans Recd
	9/2/16		Attending to work of section	Rest Recd
	10/2/16		Evacuated 10 horses & 3 mules. 8 horses & 2 mules 61st Div. Also 1st R.H.A.S.C member in Army 262 & mother to LEC	Ans Recd
	11/2/16		Attend to work of section	Ans Recd
	12/2/16		Attending to work of section	Ans Recd
	13/2/16		Evacuated 16 horses & 3 mules. 8 horses & 2 mules belonging to 61st Div	Ans Recd
	14/2/16		Attending to work of section	Ans Recd
	15/2/16		Evacuated 10 horses & 2 mules. 6 horses & 2 mules belonging to 61st Div	Ans Recd
	16/2/16		Evacuated 32 horses belonging to 31st Div & 61st Div	Ans Recd

Army Form C. 2118.

WAR DIARY
or
INTELLIGENCE SUMMARY.
(Erase heading not required.)

Instructions regarding War Diaries and Intelligence Summaries are contained in F.S. Regs., Part II. and the Staff Manual respectively. Title pages will be prepared in manuscript.

Place	Date	Hour	Summary of Events and Information	Remarks and references to Appendices
MARTINSART	1/7		Evacuated 10 horses & 2 mules	Aux Pers
"	2/7		Attended to work of Section	Aux Pers
"	3/7		Evacuated 16 horses & 4 mules	Aux Pers
"	4/7		Evacuated 22 horses & 5 mules	Aux Pers
"	5/7		Attended to work of Section. Capt Brown to meet reports from 30 M.V.S.	Aux Pers
"	6/7		Evacuated 38 horses & 1 mule	Aux Pers
"	7/7		Attended to work of Section	Aux Pers
"	8/7		Evacuated 33 horses & 7 mules 18 horses & 7 mules belonging to 61 Div	Aux Pers
"	9/7		Attended to work of Section	Aux Pers
"	10/7		Evacuated 25 horses 17 horses belonging to 61 Div	Aux Pers
"	11/7		Attended to work of Section	Aux Pers
"	12/7		Evacuated 31 horses & 1 mule 17 horses & 1 mule belonging to 61 Div	Aux Pers
"	13/7		Attended to work of Section	Aux Pers
"	14/7		Evacuated 33 horses & 4 mules 24 horses & 1 mule belonging to 61 Div	Aux Pers
"	15/7		Attended to work of Section	Aux Pers
"	16/7		Marched from Martinsart to Marieux. Left unit 30 M.V.S. 22 horses & 7 mules 6 horses & 7 mules belonging to 61 Div. L/Cpl Green, Pte Johns, Harper, Hart & Stalker left unit. Sgt. Gibbs, Cpl. Scarr, S/S Hardwick rejoined	Aux Pers

T2134. Wt. W708-776. 500000. 4/15. Sir J. C. & B.

Army Form C. 2118.

WAR DIARY
or
INTELLIGENCE SUMMARY.
(Erase heading not required.)

Instructions regarding War Diaries and Intelligence Summaries are contained in F. S. Regs., Part II. and the Staff Manual respectively. Title pages will be prepared in manuscript.

Place	Date	Hour	Summary of Events and Information	Remarks and references to Appendices
MARIEUX	17/7		Left Marieux 8 am arrived BERNAVILLE 9.30 am	AnRes
BERNAVILLE	18/7		At Bernaville	AnRes
	19/7		Left Bernaville 8.30 am arrived at NEUVILLE 11.30 am	AnRes
NEUVILLE	20/7		Attended to rest of section. 1st Farriers reported for duty	AnRes
	21/7		Attended to rest of section. 1st Gibbs reported for duty	AnRes
	22/7		Attended to rest of section	AnRes
	23/7		Attended to rest of section	AnRes
	24/7		Attended to rest of section	AnRes
	25/7		Attended to rest of section	AnRes
	26/7		Attended to rest of section. L. Cpl Green, Pte Broken, Pte Dooley reported & Ptes Haynes reported.	AnRes
	27/7		Attended to rest of section. 3 crosses sent to m. Ledgence Co. 15 for	AnRes
	28/7		Attended to rest of section	AnRes
	29/7		Attended to rest of section	AnRes
	30/7		Evacuated 2 Grey horses belonging to 61 Div to one to Abbeville	AnRes
	31/7		Evacuated 3 horses to one to Abbeville, belonging to 61 Div	AnRes

T2134. Wt. W708—776. 500000. 4/15. Sir J. C. & S.

Army Form C. 2118.

WAR DIARY
or
INTELLIGENCE SUMMARY.
(Erase heading not required.)

Instructions regarding War Diaries and Intelligence Summaries are contained in F. S. Regs., Part II. and the Staff Manual respectively. Title pages will be prepared in manuscript.

21st S.M. MOBILE VETERINARY SECTION
61st DIVISION

Place	Date	Hour	Summary of Events and Information	Remarks and references to Appendices
NEUVILLE	1/7		Evacuated 2 horses & 1 mule & 3 horses & 1 mule belonging to 61 Div	Cert Res
	2/7		Evacuated 22 horses & 1 mule belonging to 61 Div	Cert Res
	3/7		Evacuated 49 horses & 1lb mules belonging to 61 Div & Carcass sold to M Fougere fr 30 fr	Cert Res
	4/7		Marched from Neuville to LONGPRE	Cert Res
LONGPRE	5/7		Attended to sick of section	Cert Res
	6/7		Attended to sick of section	Cert Res
	7/7		Attended to sick of section	Cert Res
	8/7		Attended to sick of section	Cert Res
	9/7		Attended to sick of section	Cert Res
	10/7		Attended to sick of section	Cert Res / Cert Res
	11/7		Evacuated 20 horses & 2 mules belonging to 61 Div	Cert Res
	12/7		Evacuated 1 horse belonging to 61 Div	
	13/7		Attended to sick of section	Cert Res
	14/7		Marched from Longpre to ARGOEUVES	Cert Res
GOEUVES	15/7		Marched from Argoeuves to AUDIGNY	Cert Res
AUDIGNY	16/7		Marched from Audigny to MANGARD	Cert Res

T2134. Wt. W708–776. 500000. 4/15. Sir J. C. & S.

Army Form C. 2118.

WAR DIARY
or
INTELLIGENCE SUMMARY.
(Erase heading not required.)

Vol 10

Place	Date	Hour	Summary of Events and Information	Remarks and references to Appendices
HANGARD	17/2/17		Handed over to 2,3 & Capt Blosom	Rogers
"	18/2/17		Attended to work of Section	G.W.Blosom
"	19/2/17		Section moved to HARBONNIÈRES	G.W.Blosom
HARBONNIÈRES	20/2/17		Attended to duties of Section	G.W.Blosom
"	21/2/17		Attended to duties of Section	G.W.Blosom
"	22/2/17		Attended to duties of Section	G.W.Blosom
"	23/2/17		Attended to duties of Section	G.W.Blosom
"	24/2/17		Attended to duties of Section	G.W.Blosom
"	25/2/17		Attended to duties of Section	G.W.Blosom
"	26/2/17		Attended to duties of Section	G.W.Blosom
"	27/2/17		Evacuated 3 Horses and 5 Mules belonging to 61st Division	G.W.Blosom
"	28/2/17		Attended to duties of Section	G.W.Blosom

Vol XI

Army Form C. 2118.

WAR DIARY
or
INTELLIGENCE SUMMARY.
(Erase heading not required.)

Instructions regarding War Diaries and Intelligence Summaries are contained in F. S. Regs., Part II. and the Staff Manual respectively. Title pages will be prepared in manuscript.

Place	Date	Hour	Summary of Events and Information	Remarks and references to Appendices
HARBONNIERES	1/3/17		Attended to duties of Section & H.Q. Train	S.M. Bloxsome
"	2/3/17		Attended to duties of Section	S.M. Bloxsome
"	3/3/17		Attended to duties of Section destroyed one sternum and 1 horse belonging to 61st Division	S.M. Bloxsome
"	4/3/17		Attended to duties of Section, and H Div Sin Train	S.M. Bloxsome
"	5/3/17		Attended to duties of Section, and D.A.C	S.M. Bloxsome
"	6/3/17		Evacuated 13 Horses & 3 Mules belonging to 61st Division, Visited D.A.C	S.M. Bloxsome
"	7/3/17		Attended to duties of Section and D.A.C an H.Q. Train	S.M. Bloxsome
"	8/3/17		Attended to duties of Section and D.A.C. Took extra Stabling. Received 2 Stallions	S.M. Bloxsome
"	9/3/17		Attended to duties of Section, D.A.C & Train Carted material for improvement /Horse Stables	S.M. Bloxsome
"	10/3/17		Attended to duties of Section & D.A.C. Evacuated 6 Mules & 2 Horses belonging to 61st Division	S.M. Bloxsome
"	11/3/17		Attended to duties of Section D.A.C & H.Q. Train	S.M. Bloxsome
"	12/3/17		Attended to duties of Section & D.A.C. Carted material for improvement of Horse Stables	S.M. Bloxsome
"	13/3/17		Attended to duties of Section & D.A.C. Carted material for improvement of Horse Stables	S.M. Bloxsome
"	14/3/17		Attended to duties of Section & D.A.C & H.Q. Train	S.M. Bloxsome
"	15/3/17		Attended to duties of Section & D.A.C. relaying floor of Stables of Section	S.M. Bloxsome
"	16/3/17		Attended to duties of Section, D.A.C. and Div Train	S.M. Bloxsome

Army Form C. 2118.

WAR DIARY
or
INTELLIGENCE SUMMARY.
(Erase heading not required.)

Instructions regarding War Diaries and Intelligence Summaries are contained in F.S. Regs., Part II. and the Staff Manual respectively. Title pages will be prepared in manuscript.

Place	Date	Hour	Summary of Events and Information	Remarks and references to Appendices
HARBONNIERES	17/3/17		Evacuated 16 Horses belonging to 61st Division	G.M.Bloxsome
"	18/3/17		Division received orders to move. Standing to. Attended to duties of Section, AMC & A.V. Corps	G.M.Bloxsome
"	19/3/17		Attended to duties of Section	G.M.Bloxsome
"	20/3/17		Evacuated 3 Mules & 12 Horses belonging to 61st Division & 1 belonging to other than 61st Division	G.M.Bloxsome
	21/3/17		Attended to duties of Section	G.M.Bloxsome
	22/3/17		Attended to duties of Section	G.M.Bloxsome
	23/3/17		Attended to duties of Section	G.M.Bloxsome
	24/3/17		Attended to duties of Section, located and arranged for advance aid Post at Omiécourt	G.M.Bloxsome
	25/3/17		Attended to duties of Section	G.M.Bloxsome
	26/3/17		Attended to duties of Section	G.M.Bloxsome
	27/3/17		Evacuated 23 Horses & 1 Mule belonging to 61st Division, received advance Pt.	G.M.Bloxsome
	28/3/17		Section moved to Omiécourt	G.M.Bloxsome
OMIECOURT	29/3/17		Section moved to Y	G.M.Bloxsome
Y	30/3/17		Attended to duties of Section, and improved end of Billets	G.M.Bloxsome
Y	31/3/17		Attended to duties of Section and inspected 142 Strength at Pargny	G.M.Bloxsome
	1/4/17			

WAR DIARY
or
INTELLIGENCE SUMMARY.
(Erase heading not required.)

Army Form C. 2118.

Instructions regarding War Diaries and Intelligence Summaries are contained in F. S. Regs., Part II. and the Staff Manual respectively. Title pages will be prepared in manuscript.

MOBILE VETERINARY SECTION
No............
Date............
61st DIVISION

Place	Date	Hour	Summary of Events and Information	Remarks and references to Appendices
BILLONCOURT.	16/7		Attended duties of Section	G.H. Blossom
"	17/7		Evacuated 13 Horses & 3 Mules belonging to 61st Division	G.H. Blossom
"	18/7		Attended to duties of Section, visited D.C.I., and Donilly, arranged with No. 32 M.V.S. re taking over	G.H. Blossom
"	19/7		Attended to duties of Section	G.H. Blossom
"	20/7		Attended to duties of Section	G.H. Blossom
"	21/7		Evacuated 9 Horses & 2 Mules, belonging to 61st Division	G.H. Blossom
DOUILLY	22/7		Section moved from BILLONCOURT to DOUILLY	G.H. Blossom
"	23/7		Attended to duties of Section, cleaned up billets & farmyard Standings	G.H. Blossom
"	24/7		Attended to duties of Section, visited D.C.I. Inspected Billets & Coy. 3 men attached	G.H. Blossom
"	25/7		Attended duties of Section, fair timber & erected passage to roof in Section Stable	G.H. Blossom
"	26/7		Attended duties of Section, visited C.A.M. Section D.A.C. 1st & 2nd F.A. Completed roof in J. Stable	G.H. Blossom
"	27/7		Attended duties of Section, Erected Saddle Room.	G.H. Blossom
"	28/7		Evacuated 5 Horses belonging to other Units of 61st Division, visited D.C.L.I.	G.H. Blossom
"	29/7		Attended duties of Section, visited D.A.C. & Lieut. Hutcheon	G.H. Blossom
"	30/7		Attended duties of Section	G.H. Blossom

Army Form C. 2118.

WAR DIARY
or
INTELLIGENCE SUMMARY.
(Erase heading not required.)

Instructions regarding War Diaries and Intelligence Summaries are contained in F. S. Regs., Part II. and the Staff Manual respectively. Title pages will be prepared in manuscript.

MOBILE VETERINARY SECTION
61st DIVISION

Place	Date	Hour	Summary of Events and Information	Remarks and references to Appendices
Y	1/4/17		Attached to duties of Section & improvement of Billets	G.H. Blossom
"	2/4/17		Attached to duties of Section	G.H. Blossom
"	3/4/17		Attached to duties of Section & improvement of Billets	G.H. Blossom
"	4/4/17		Attached to duties of Section, Completed new Cast Horse & Mule Form	G.H. Blossom
"	5/4/17		Returned 8 Horses & mules to knit 61st Division Visited M.M.P & S.C.L. Completed Best Horses	G.H. Blossom
"	6/4/17		Attached to duties of Section	G.H. Blossom
"	7/4/17		Evacuated 15 Horses & one mule, 12 Horses & 1 mule belonging to 61st Division	G.H. Blossom
"	8/4/17		Attached to duties of Section & D.C.L.I.	G.H. Blossom
"	9/4/17		Attached to duties of Section, Cleaned new Standing for 15 Horses	G.H. Blossom
"	10/4/17		Evacuated 3.4 Horses & 2 Mules, 30 Horses & 2 mules belonging to 61st Division	G.H. Blossom
"	11/4/17		Attached to duties of Section and D.C.L.I.	G.H. Blossom
BILLANCOURT	12/4/17		Section and 37 Sick Horses moved to BILLANCOURT	G.H. Blossom
"	13/4/17		Attached duties of Section, Cleaned at Billet, Commenced relaying Entrance with Brick	G.H. Blossom
"	14/4/17		Evacuated 2.3 Horses & 1 Mule 61st Division, Cleared up Yard & Finished relaying Entrance Visited 1st Infantry Brigade, 1st Division	G.H. Blossom
"	15/4/17		Attached to duties of Section	G.H. Blossom

WAR DIARY
or
INTELLIGENCE SUMMARY.
(Erase heading not required.)

Army Form C. 2118.

Place	Date	Hour	Summary of Events and Information	Remarks and references to Appendices
DOUILLY.	1/5/17		Evacuated 2 Horses 61st Division, 3 Horses other Ranks 61st Division (1. Cas.)	G.H.Blasorne
"	2/5/17		Attended duties of Section Visited D.C.L.I. S.A.A. D.A.C. & F.A.	G.H.Blasorne
"	3/5/17		Attended duties of Section	G.H.Blasorne
"	4/5/17		Attended duties of Section Visited D.C.L.I., F.A. & S.A.A. Sec D.A.C.	G.H.Blasorne
"	5/5/17		Evacuated 3 Horses belonging to 61st Division & 3 Horses other Ranks 61st Division (Cas.)	G.H.Blasorne
"	6/5/17		Attended to duties of Section & improvement of surroundings.	G.H.Blasorne
"	7/5/17		Attended duties of Section Visited S.A.A. D.A.C. 2/3 F.A. and D.C.L.I. proceeded with building of stal.	G.H.Blasorne
"	8/5/17		Evacuated & transit Mule 61st Division, & transit Mule other Ranks 61st Division transferred 1 Horse (For Use) IV Corps M.V.S.	G.H.Blasorne
"	9/5/17		Attended to duties of Section, Superintending of Surroundings & finishing of stal.	G.H.Blasorne
"	10/5/17		Attended duties of Section, Visited 2/3 F.A. & S.A.A. D.A.C. proceeded with building of stal. Inspecting Harness.	G.H.Blasorne
"	11/5/17		Attended duties of Section, proceeded with building new stal. Transferred 12 Horses to IV Corps. M.V.S.	G.H.Blasorne
"	12/5/17		Evacuated 8 Horses 61st Division, 3 Mules & 2 Horses other Ranks 61st Division Visited 2/3 F.A. & S.A.A. D.A.C.	G.H.Blasorne
"	13/5/17		Attended to duties of Section	G.H.Blasorne
"	14/5/17		Attended duties of Section Transferred 23 Horses & R.G.A. to IV Corps M.V.S. Visited S.A.A. D.A.C. & 2/3 F.A.	G.H.Blasorne
BETHENCOURT.	15/5/17		Evacuated 16 Horses & 2 Mules 61st Division & 2 mules other Ranks 61st Division Horse Section to BETHENCOURT.	G.H.Blasorne
"	16/5/17		Attended to duties of Section, Shifted Billets Visited D.C.L.I. & S.A.A. D.A.C.	G.H.Blasorne

Army Form C. 2118.

WAR DIARY
or
INTELLIGENCE SUMMARY.
(Erase heading not required.)

Instructions regarding War Diaries and Intelligence Summaries are contained in F. S. Regs., Part II. and the Staff Manual respectively. Title pages will be prepared in manuscript.

MOBILE VETERINARY SECTION
No.
Date.
61st DIVISION

Place	Date	Hour	Summary of Events and Information	Remarks and references to Appendices
BETHENCOURT	15/5/17		Attend to duties of Section. Evacuated 17 gazed Horses	G.M.Blossoms
"	16/5/17		Attend to duties of Section. Evacuated 17 gazed Horses	G.M.Blossoms
"	19/5/17		Attend to duties of Section. Received 1 gazed Horse.	G.M.Blossoms
CAYEUX	20/5/17		Moved Section to CAYEUX	G.M.Blossoms
GLISSY	21/5/17		Moved Section to GLISSY	G.M.Blossoms
NAOURS	22/5/17		Moved Section to NAOURS	G.M.Blossoms
"	23/5/17		Attend to duties of Section	G.M.Blossoms
OUTREBOIS	24/5/17		Moved Section to OUTREBOIS	G.M.Blossoms
"	25/5/17		Attend to duties of Section	G.M.Blossoms
"	26/5/17		Evacuated 24 Horses belonging to 61st Division	G.M.Blossoms
"	27/5/17		Attend to duties of Section	G.M.Blossoms
"	28/5/17		Attend to duties of Section	G.M.Blossoms
"	29/5/17		Evacuated 7 Horses belonging to 61st Division. Transferred 1 Sergt & 2 men to Corps Mob. Vet. Sect.	G.M.Blossoms
"	30/5/17		Attend to duties of Section. Inspected Office.	G.M.Blossoms
"	31/5/17		Attend to duties of Section	G.M.Blossoms

Army Form C. 2118.

WAR DIARY
or
INTELLIGENCE SUMMARY.
(Erase heading not required.)

Instructions regarding War Diaries and Intelligence Summaries are contained in F. S. Regs., Part II. and the Staff Manual respectively. Title pages will be prepared in manuscript.

Place	Date	Hour	Summary of Events and Information	Remarks and references to Appendices
DUNKREBOIS.	1/6/17		Attended to duties of Section	G.M. Blossome
"	2/6/17		Evacuated 9 horses, & belonging to 61st Division	G.M. Blossome
"	3/6/17		Attended to duties of Section	G.M. Blossome
"	4/6/17		Attended to duties of Section	G.M. Blossome
"	5/6/17		Attended to duties of Section	G.M. Blossome
"	6/6/17		Attended to duties of Section	G.M. Blossome
"	7/6/17		Attended to duties of Section. Evacuated 5 horses belonging to 61st Division (Mange Suspect)	G.M. Blossome
L'ARBRET	8/6/17		Attended to duties of Section, Moved Section to L'ARBRET	G.M. Blossome
WARLUS.	9/6/17		Moved Section to WARLUS. Cleaned Billets	G.M. Blossome
"	10/6/17		Attended to duties of Section & improvement of Billets	G.M. Blossome
"	11/6/17		Attended to duties of Section	G.M. Blossome
"	12/6/17		Moved Section to AGNEZ-les-DUISANS.	G.M. Blossome
AGNEZ-les-DUISANS	13/6/17		Evacuated 14 horses 12, belonging to 61st Division	G.M. Blossome
"	14/6/17		Attended duties of Section, Castor check for horses held over for charge of 182	G.M. Blossome
"	14/6/17		Inspect of M.G. Sec, 2 F.A. 476 F.G.R.E. Wire Co Train	G.M. Blossome
"	15/6/17		All cases taken by Section thence to Mob 12nd F.A. & Subriched Co Lt Division	G.M. Blossome

T2134. Wt. W708-776. 500000. 4/15. Sir J. C. & S.

Army Form C. 2118.

WAR DIARY
or
INTELLIGENCE SUMMARY.
(Erase heading not required.)

Instructions regarding War Diaries and Intelligence Summaries are contained in F. S. Regs., Part II. and the Staff Manual respectively. Title pages will be prepared in manuscript.

Place	Date	Hour	Summary of Events and Information	Remarks and references to Appendices
AGNEZ-LES-DUISANS	16/7/17		Evacuated 27 Horses & 4 Mules belonging to 61st Div. & 1 Horse of Cav/Has. 61st allowed duties of Section Units	G.H.Blossom
"	17/7/17		Attended to duties of Section Units	G.H.Blossom
"	18/7/17		Evacuated 21 Horses belonging to 61st Division	G.H.Blossom
"	19/7/17		Attended duties of Section & Units of 61st and to Divisions	G.H.Blossom
"	20/7/17		Evacuated 10 Horses belonging to 61st Division. Investigated cases of either horse and Have been damaged by troops at BARLY. Allowed duties of section to the Units	G.H.Blossom G.H.Blossom
REBREUVIETTE	21/7/17		Attended duties of Section, packed up, cleaned Billet.	G.H.Blossom
"	22/7/17		Moved Section to REBREUVIETTE	G.H.Blossom
VIEIL-HESDIN	23/7/17		Moved Section to VIEIL-HESDIN.	G.H.Blossom
"	24/7/17		Attended duties of Section received Billet at HERMEL	G.H.Blossom
HERMEL	25/7/17		Moved Section to HERMEL	G.H.Blossom
"	26/7/17		Attended duties of Section Vehicles & Units.	G.H.Blossom
"	27/7/17		Evacuated 3 Horses belonging 61st Division & 2 Mules (Strays)	G.H.Blossom
"	28/7/17		Attended duties of Section Units	G.H.Blossom
"	29/7/17		Attended duties of Section Units	G.H.Blossom
"	30/7/17		Evacuated 3 Horses & 1 Mule belonging 61st Division, also 1 Mule Stray	G.H.Blossom

WAR DIARY
or
INTELLIGENCE SUMMARY.
(Erase heading not required.)

Army Form C. 2118.

Vol 15

Place	Date	Hour	Summary of Events and Information	Remarks and references to Appendices
HERNEL	1/7/17		Attended duties of Section Unit.	Fh. Blossoms.
"	2/7/17		Evacuated 13 horses & 6 Mules (13 horses & 5 Mules belonging 61st Division, 1 Mule West Surbury)	Fh. Blossoms.
"	3/7/17		Attended duties of Section Unit.	Fh. Blossoms.
"	4/7/17		Evacuated 28 horses & 6 Mules belonging to 37th Division and 3 horses belonging 61st Division	Fh. Blossoms.
"	5/7/17		Attended duties of Section & other Units	Fh. Blossoms.
"	6/7/17		Attended duties of Section & other Units	Fh. Blossoms.
"	7/7/17		Evacuated 6 horses belonging to 61st Division, attended duties of Section & other Units	Fh. Blossoms.
"	8/7/17		Attended duties of Section	Fh. Possum.
"	9/7/17		Proceeded England on Leave Authority Warrant. B.186618.	Ow
"	10/7/17			
"	10/7/17		Evacuated by A.D.V.S. 4 horses belonging to 61st Division	Leave
"	12/7/17			
"	13/7/17			
"	14/7/17		Evacuated by A.D.V.S. 5 horses & 1 Mule, (3 horses & 1 Mule belonging to 61st Division)	to
"	15/7/17			
"	16/7/17			20.7.17.

Army Form C. 2118.

WAR DIARY
or
INTELLIGENCE SUMMARY.
(Erase heading not required.)

Instructions regarding War Diaries and Intelligence Summaries are contained in F. S. Regs., Part II. and the Staff Manual respectively. Title pages will be prepared in manuscript.

MOBILE VETERINARY SECTION — No. — Date 1-8-17 — 61st DIVISION

Place	Date	Hour	Summary of Events and Information	Remarks and references to Appendices
HERMEL	17/7/17			OV
"	18/7/17		Evacuated by A.D.V.S 4 Horses & 2 Mules belonging to 61st Division	Leave
"	19.7.17			
"	20.7.17			
"	21.7.17		Evacuated to A.D.V.S. 4 Horses + 1 Mule (5 Horses and 1 Mule belonging to 61st Division)	
"	21.7.17		Returned from Leave.	G. M. Blossome
"	22.7.17		Attended duties of Section & other Units	G.M. Blossome
"	23.7.17		Attended to duties of Section, Rifle Inspection & Parade for Pay	G.M. Blossome
"	24.7.17		Transferred 9 horses & 1 Mule belonging to 61st Division & 1 Horse other than 61st Division to 9th Cavalry Division M.V.S.	G.M. Blossome
"	25.7.17		Attended duties of section, and inspection, packing & preparing to move.	G.M. Blossome
"	26.7.17		Entrained at FREVENT for BAVINCHOVE thence by road to ERKELSBRUGGE	G.M. Blossome
ERKELSBRUGGE	27.7.17		Attended to duties of Section, cleaned up Billets	G.M. Blossome
"	28.7.17		Attended to duties of Section, visited 4 other Units.	G.M. Blossome
"	29.7.17		Attended to duties of Section, P.M. of R.R. Wm. R. Visited NIELLES, WATTEN, MILLAIN & ZENEGHEM in relief of EM & Coster.	G.M. Blossome

WAR DIARY
or
INTELLIGENCE SUMMARY.

Army Form C. 2118.

Place	Date	Hour	Summary of Events and Information	Remarks and references to Appendices
ERNEIS BRUGGE 30/7			All Ensted to duties of Section & other Units	Gt Blossom
"	31/7		Attached to duties of Section, Corps & other Units	Gt Blossom

Army Form C. 2118.

WAR DIARY
or
INTELLIGENCE SUMMARY.
(Erase heading not required.)

Vol 16

Place	Date	Hour	Summary of Events and Information	Remarks and references to Appendices
POPERINGHE	26/8/17		Attended to duties of Section & other Units	G.W.Blossom.
"	27/8/17		Attended duties of Section & other Units	G.W.Blossom
"	28/8/17		Attended duties of Section & other Units. Visited Corps Mob Vet & arranged re Evacuation	G.W.Blossom
"	29/8/17		Evacuated 16 Horses & 7 Mules belonging to 61st Division, 15 Horses & 13 Mules O/U. Had 61st Division by road to Corps Mob Vet, vol/Veteries attended duties of Section	G.W.Blossom
"	30/8/17		Attended to duties of Section, took in 59 Cases.	G.W.Blossom
"	31/8/17		Attended to duties of Section & other Units, took in 34 Cases, Evacuated 49 Horses & 3 Mules, (7) Horses belonging to 61st Division.	G.W.Blossom.

Army Form C. 2118.

WAR DIARY or INTELLIGENCE SUMMARY.

(Erase heading not required.)

Instructions regarding War Diaries and Intelligence Summaries are contained in F. S. Regs., Part II. and the Staff Manual respectively. Title pages will be prepared in manuscript.

MOBILE VETERINARY SECTION
No. ....
Date 31-8-17
61st DIVISION

Place	Date	Hour	Summary of Events and Information	Remarks and references to Appendices
POPERINGHE	15/8/17		Moved Section to POPERINGHE, Camped in Field.	G.M. Blossome
"	16/8/17		Attended duties of Section, Sent N.C.O. + 3 men mounted to XIX Corps Vet Mob. Detachment	G.M. Blossome
"	17/8/17		Attended duties of Section, Visited 36 M. Mob. Vet. Sec., & arranged to take over Mobile Aid Post, Sent N.C.O. + 1 man to take over.	G.M. Blossome
"	18/8/17		Took over from 36th Mob. Vet. Sec. at G.M.A. + 6 M/wdw duties of Section, other units & 24 Labour Co, Moored Section	G.M. Blossome
"	19/8/17		Attended duties of Section & Units, Visited Aid Post. Evacuated 18 Horses, other Krans 61st Division, to X.I.X Corps Mob. Vet. Detachment. Discharged 5 + thy grants.	G.M. Blossome
"	20/8/17		Attended to duties of Section & Units Evacuated 1 Foot Case (Horse) other Ran 61st Division	G.M. Blossome
"	21/8/17		Attended to duties of Section & Units discharged 4 thy grants. Evacuated 30 horses + 1 Mule (6 horses belonging to 61st Division), Evacuated 1 Foot Case, other Ran Grehi.	G.M. Blossome
"	22/8/17		Attended duties of Section & Units. Evacuated 76 Horses + 29 Mules (4 horses + 2 Mules belonging to 61st Division.	G.M. Blossome
"	23/8/17		Attended to duties of Section & Units. Evacuated 1 Horse + 1 Mule (Field Case) Other Ran 6th Div.	G.M. Blossome
"	24/8/17		Attended to duties of Section & Units, attached A.H.Q. + Mobile XIX Corps M/Vd Det	G.M. Blossome
"	25/8/17		Attended to duties of Section, 2 men & horses reported limit from XIX Corps Mob. Detachment	G.M. Blossome

WAR DIARY
or
INTELLIGENCE SUMMARY.
(Erase heading not required.)

Army Form C. 2118.

Place	Date	Hour	Summary of Events and Information	Remarks and references to Appendices
ERKELSBRUGGE	1/8/17		Attended to duties of Section of the Unit	
"	2/8/17		Attended to duties of Section of Unit	Ly Blackburn
"	3/8/17		Attended to duties of Section of Unit. Evacuated 11 Horses by Road to STOMER (2 Mob Vet 61st Division)	Ly Blackburn
"	4/8/17		Attended to duties of Section of Unit. Examined 1 Mare & 9 Cattle for Mr Baquart Lockent, BOLLZEELE	Ly Blackburn
"	5/8/17		Drive to Sale.	Ly Blackburn
"	6/8/17		Attended to duties of Section of the Unit.	Ly Blackburn
"	7/8/17		Attended to duties of Section of the Unit. VIII Corps Troops.	Ly Blackburn
"	8/8/17		Attended to duties of Section to the Unit Cattle & Horse belonging to 3rd & 5th Divisions. Evacuated by 61st Division	Ly Blackburn
"	9/8/17		Move to STOMER 11 Horses & 1 Mule belonging to 61st Division	Ly Blackburn
"	10/8/17		Attended to duties of Section to the Unit	Ly Blackburn
"	11/8/17		Attended to duties of Section to the Unit. PM a Pig N Dr & 2/6 Manch Regt.	Ly Blackburn
"	12/8/17		Attended to duties of Section to the Unit	Ly Blackburn
"	13/8/17		Attended to duties of Section to the Unit. Evacuated 6 Horses & road to STOMER 61st Division	Ly Blackburn
"	14/8/17		Attended to duties of Section to the Unit. Collected 1 Horse Stolen by Reservist in Military	Ly Blackburn
"	15/8/17		Attended to duties of Section of the Unit. VIII Corps Troops to 11 Corps School.	Ly Blackburn
"	16/8/17		Attended to duties of Section to the Unit. Evacuated 2 Horses 61st Division by road to STOMER	Ly Blackburn

WAR DIARY
or
INTELLIGENCE SUMMARY.

Army Form C. 2118.

(Erase heading not required.)

Place	Date	Hour	Summary of Events and Information	Remarks and references to Appendices
POPERINGHE	1/9/17		Attended to duties of Section to the Units took in 21 Cases. Evacuated 38 horses & 2 Mules other than 61st Division	G.W. Blossome
"	2/9/17		Attended to duties of Section to the Units. Took in 112 Cases, Evacuated 1 Horse (Float Case) other than 61st Division	G.W. Blossome
"	3/9/17		Attended to duties of Section to the Units admitted 57 Cases, Evacuated by Road to SYOMER 8 8 Horses & 5 Mules, (64 Horses & 5 Mules belonging to 61st Division) Evacuated 1 Horse other than 61st Division to Corps Mob. Detachment (XIX) Float Case	G.W. Blossome
"	4/9/17		Attended to duties of Section to the Units, admitted 36 Cases, Destroyed & buried 1, Evacuated to XIX Corps Mobile Detachment 24 Horses and 22 Mules, (7 Horses & 9 Mules belonging to 61st Division) (2 Float Cases)	G.W. Blossome
"	5/9/17		Evacuated 43 Horses and 14 Mules (1 Float Case) to XIX Corps Mobile Detachment (4 Horses & 7 Mules belonging to 61st Division.)	G.M. Blossome
"	6/9/17		Attended to the duties of Section & Units Admitted 25 Cases. Attended to duties of Section, picket L.L. Pat. & 21 I.I. Fork in 10 Cases, Evacuated 14 horses & 9 Mules. (6 horses & 2 Mules belonging to 61st Division.)	G.M. Blossome

(Mobile Veterinary Section stamp, Date 1-10-17, 61st Division)

Army Form C. 2118.

WAR DIARY
or
INTELLIGENCE SUMMARY.
(Erase heading not required.)

Instructions regarding War Diaries and Intelligence Summaries are contained in F.S. Regs., Part II. and the Staff Manual respectively. Title pages will be prepared in manuscript.

MOBILE VETERINARY SECTION
61st DIVISION
Date 1-10-17

Place	Date	Hour	Summary of Events and Information	Remarks and references to Appendices
POPERINGHE	7/9/17		Admitted 18 Cases. Evacuated 9 Horses & 4 Mules (6 Horses & 3 Mules belonging to 61st Div.) (1 Fatal Case) Attached to book of Section & other Units. Earthed over 1 Manure Dump.	G.W.Blaxsome
"	8/9/17		Attended to duties of Section & other Units, admitted 19 Cases, earthed over Manure Dump & Generally cleaned up billets, returned one.	G.W.Blaxsome
"	9/9/17		Attended to duties of Section & Units admitted 10 Cases.	G.W.Blaxsome
"	10/9/17		Attended to duties of Section & Units admitted 23 Cases.	G.W.Blaxsome
"	11/9/17		Attended to duties of Section & Units admitted 12 Cases Destroyed one	G.W.Blaxsome
"	12/9/17		Attended to duties of Section & Units admitted 23 Cases Evacuated 30 Horses & 9 Mules by Road to I'OMER (5 Horses & 9 Mules belonging to 61st Division) Drehaqui & Proviene 2 Horses (One 61st Division)	G.W.Blaxsome
"	13/9/17		Attended duties of Section & Units. Admitted 10 Cases, Evacuated 1 Horse other than 61st Division by Road to Rail Siding.	G.W.Blaxsome
"	14/9/17		Attended duties of Section. Evacuated 23 Horses & 7 Mules (9 Horses & 3 Mules belonging to 61st Division) by road to Corps Mob. Vet. Rail Siding.	G.W.Blaxsome
WATOU	15/9/17		Moved Section to No 2 Area WATOU & handed over to MOB. VET. SEC. 55th DIVISION.	G.W.Blaxsome
"	16/9/17		Attended to duties of Section	G.W.Blaxsome

WAR DIARY
or
INTELLIGENCE SUMMARY.
(Erase heading not required.)

Army Form C. 2118.

Instructions regarding War Diaries and Intelligence Summaries are contained in F. S. Regs., Part II. and the Staff Manual respectively. Title pages will be prepared in manuscript.

MOBILE VETERINARY SECTION
No.
Date 1 – 10 –17
81st DIVISION

Place	Date	Hour	Summary of Events and Information	Remarks and references to Appendices
WORMHOUDT	17/9/17		Moved Section to I.18.a.9.1. Barre WORMHOUDT	G.W. Blossom
"	18/9/17		Altered duties of Section, reconnoitred route to Station.	G.W. Blossom
WANQUETIN	19/9/17		Moved Section to WANQUETIN.	G.W. Blossom
AGNEZ-LEZ-DUISANS	20/9/17		Moved Section to AGNEZ-LEZ-DUISANS	G.W. Blossom
"	21/9/17		Altered duties of Section, made P.M. on Mules 479 Field Co R.E., visited Situation of coming mob, arranged with O.C. 17th Div. M.06 Vet Sec. re taking over.	G.W. Blossom
"	22/9/17		Attended to duties of Section to other Units.	G.W. Blossom
"	23/9/17		Attended to duties of Section to other Units.	G.W. Blossom
"	24/9/17		Attended to duties of Section to other Units, prepared for move, Staff Sergt. & 2 men to take over XVII Corps Horse Disp.	G.W. Blossom
ARRAS G.13.d.8.5	25/9/17		Moved Section to G.13.d.8.5. Settled in to Billets. Took over XVII Corps Dipping Station.	G.W. Blossom
			Strength with M.o.B. Vet Sec from 17th Division.	G.W. Blossom
"	26/9/17		Attended to duties of Section, Interviewed Lt Col Pottin. Lt Col Lake.	G.W. Blossom
"	27/9/17		Issued 27 Horse Surplus of 180 "Kahun Group" Brook Horse sick & Wounded, attended duties of Section & Units.	G.W. Blossom

Army Form C. 2118.

WAR DIARY
or
INTELLIGENCE SUMMARY.

Place	Date	Hour	Summary of Events and Information	Remarks and references to Appendices
(ARRAS) G.13.d.8.5	28.9.17		Attached to work of Section to other Units.	G.W.Bourne
"	29.9.17		Evacuated 23 Horses & 8 Mules (4 horses & 5 mules belonging to 61st Division) attached to work of Section to other Units.	G.W.Bourne
"	30.9.17		Attached to duties of Section to other Units.	G.W.Bourne

WAR DIARY
or
INTELLIGENCE SUMMARY.
(Erase heading not required.)

Army Form C. 2118.

Vol 18

Place	Date	Hour	Summary of Events and Information	Remarks and references to Appendices
G.13d.8.5 ARRAS-ST POL	1/7		Attended duties of Section, Hors. Dip & other Units	G.W.Bissonne
"	2/7		Attended duties of Section, Horse Dip, & other Units.	G.W.Bissonne
"	3/7		Evacuated 33 Horses and 19 Mules (24 Horses & 11 Mules belonging to 61st Division, attended other duties of Section & Units	G.W.Bissonne
"	4/7		Attended duties of Section & Corps Horse Dip	G.W.Bissonne
"	5/7		Attended Duties of Section & Corps Horse Dep.	G.W.Bissonne
"	6/7		Evacuated 20 Horses all belonging to 61st Division, attended other duties of Section, Units & D.A.D.V.S., & Horse Dip	G.W.Bissonne
"	7/7		Attended to duties of Section, Units, & D.A.D.V.S., & Horse Dip	G.W.Bissonne
"	8/7		Attended to duties of Section, Units, D.A.D.V.S., & Horse Dip	G.W.Bissonne
"	9/7		Visited Lewis B.H.Q. Signals, attended duties of Section, Units, D.A.D.V.S. & Dip	G.W.Bissonne
"	10/7		Evacuated 9 Horses & 5 Mules (7 Horses & 5 Mules belonging to 61st Division), 1 Horse killed & 3 wounded in truck by Shell at Station Yard (ARRAS) attended duties of Section, Units, D.A.D.V.S. & Horse Dip	G.W.Bissonne
"	11/7		Attended duties of Section, Units, D.A.D.V.S. & Horse Dip	G.W.Bissonne
"	12/7		Attended duties of Section, Units, D.A.D.V.S. & Horse Dip.	G.W.Bissonne
"	13/7		Evacuated 7 Horses & 1 Mule (3 Horses & 1 Mule belonging to 61st Division), attended other duties of Section, Units, D.A.D.V.S. & Horse Dip	G.W.Bissonne

WAR DIARY
or
INTELLIGENCE SUMMARY.

Army Form C. 2118.

Place	Date	Hour	Summary of Events and Information	Remarks and references to Appendices
ARRAS J.POL	14/10/17		Attended duties of Section Unit, D.A.D.V.S & Arras Dip	G.W.Blaxone
"	15/10/17		Attended duties of Section, Improvement of Billets, also duties of other Units, D.A.D.V.S & Horse Dip.	G.W.Blaxone
"	16/10/17		Attended to duties of Section, Unit, D.A.D.V.S & Horse Dip.	G.W.Blaxone
"	17/10/17		Attended to duties of Section Unit, D.A.D.V.S & Horse Dip. Evacuated 11 Horses & 1 Mule (9 Horses & 1 Mule belonging to 61st Division	G.W.Blaxone
"	18/10/17		Attended to duties of Section Unit, D.A.D.V.S & Horse Dip, Conference of V.O's	G.W.Blaxone
"	19/10/17		Started orts to D.A.D.V.S, attended duties of Section, Units & Arras Dip, hauled bricks for improvement of Billets.	G.W.Blaxone
"	20/10/17		Evacuated 11 horses (9 belonging to 61st Division), attended duties of Section, Units & Horse Dip, hauled bricks for improvement of Billets.	G.W.Blaxone
"	21/10/17		Attended to duties of Section Units & Horse Dip.	G.W.Blaxone
"	22/10/17		Attended to duties of Section Units & Horse Dip, hauled Bricks for improvement of Billets	G.W.Blaxone
"	23/10/17		Attended to duties of Section Units & Arras Dip, hauled Bricks for improvement of Billets	G.W.Blaxone
"	24/10/17		Evacuated 6 Horses & 2 Mules belonging to 61st Division, Attended other duties of Section, Units & Arras Dip, hauled bricks for improvement of Billets-	G.W.Blaxone

Army Form C. 2118.

WAR DIARY
or
INTELLIGENCE SUMMARY.
(Erase heading not required.)

Instructions regarding War Diaries and Intelligence Summaries are contained in F. S. Regs., Part II. and the Staff Manual respectively. Title pages will be prepared in manuscript.

Place	Date	Hour	Summary of Events and Information	Remarks and references to Appendices
Arras 5th Pos	25/10/17		Attended duties of Section Unit & Horse Dip, Attended Cokence of V.O's, hauled Bricks &	G.W.B.
"	26/10/17		proceeded with party to huts.	
"			Monthly Inspection of Section by Col Lake ADVS XVII Corps, attended duties of Section & Horse Dip.	G.W.B.
"	27/10/17		Evacuated 6 Horses belonging to 61st Division, Issued Bricks, Issued improved Bit etc.	G.W.B.
"	28/10/17		Attended duties of Section Unit & Horse Dip	G.W.B.
"	29/10/17		Attended to duties of Section Units, Horse Dip	G.W.B.
"	30/10/17		Attended to duties of Section Unit, Horse Dip, Issued Bricks tie-pieces Bits etc	G.W.B.
"	31/10/17		Attended to duties of Section Unit, Horse Dip, Issued Bricks	G.W.B.
"			Evacuated 5 Horses 3 belonging to 61st Division, Attended to duties of Section Unit & Horse Dip.	G.W.B.

WAR DIARY or INTELLIGENCE SUMMARY

Army Form C. 2118

Mot Vety

J.V./19

Place	Date	Hour	Summary of Events and Information	Remarks and references to Appendices
ARRAS-ST POL	1/7/19		Attended duties of Section, Unit Abrades, drew bricks & improved Billets.	G.W.B.
"	2/7/19		Attended duties of Section, Unit & Horse Disp.	G.W.B.
"	3/7/19		Evacuated 3 Horses & 13 Mules belonging to 61st Division, attended other duties	
"			of Section, Unit & Horse Disp.	G.W.B.
"	4/7/19		Attended to duties of Section, Unit & Horse Bricks, improved Billets.	G.W.B.
"	5/7/19		Attended to duties of Section, Unit. Repairs to Horse Disp. Sulphur Chamber,	
"			Used Cinders for improvement of Billets.	G.W.B.
"	6/7/19		Attended to duties of Section, Units & Horse Disp. Used Cinders & improved Billets	G.W.B.
"	7/7/19		Attended to duties of Section, Horse Disp.	G.W.B.
"	8/7/19		Attended to duties of Section, Units & Horse Disp.	G.W.B.
"	9/7/19		Evacuated 11 Horses & 1 Mule, 9 Horses & 1 Mule belonging 61st Division, attended other duties	
"			of Section, Unit & Horse Disp. Other Cinders & improved Billets.	G.W.B.
"	10/7/19		Attended to duties of Section, Units, improved Horse Disp. & Billets.	G.W.B.
"	11/7/19		Attended to duties of Section, Units & Horse Disp.	G.W.B.
"	12/7/19		Evacuated 3 Horses & 2 Mules, 1 Horse & 1 Mule belonging to 61st Division, & 1 Officer's Charger	
"	13/7/19		to Ottervile, Attended to duties of Section & Horse Disp.	G.W.B.

Army Form C. 2118.

WAR DIARY
or
INTELLIGENCE SUMMARY.
(Erase heading not required.)

Instructions regarding War Diaries and Intelligence Summaries are contained in F.S. Regs., Part II. and the Staff Manual respectively. Title pages will be prepared in manuscript.

Places	Date	Hour	Summary of Events and Information	Remarks and references to Appendices
ARRAS TBL	13/7/16		Attended duties of Section. Inis & Horse Dip & reinforcement of Billets.	G.W.B.
"	14/7/16		Attended duties of Section, Inis & Horse Dip, Manoeuvres	G.W.B.
"	15/7/16		Attended duties of Section, Inis & Horse Dip. Improved Billets.	G.W.B.
"	16/7/16		Evacuated 6 Horses & belonging to 61st Division, Attended duties of Section & Dip.	G.W.B.
"	17/7/16		Attended to duties of Section Inis & Horse Dip. Carried on with Improvement of Billets	G.W.B.
"	18/7/16		Attended to duties of Section, Inis. Dug one new Sump & cleared out other at Horse Dip	G.W.B.
"	19/7/16		Evacuated 10 Horses & 2 Mules, 9 horses & 2 Mules belonging to 61st Division, Attended other duties of Section & Horse Dip.	G.W.B.
"	20/7/16		Attended duties of Section Inis & Horse Dip. Improved Surroundings of Dip.	G.W.B.
"	21/7/16		Attended duties of Section, Inis & Horse Dip, proceeded with fascine road at Dip.	G.W.B.
"	22/7/16		Attended to duties of Section Inis & Horse Dip. Improved Surroundings of Dip.	G.W.B.
"	23/7/16		Evacuated 2 Horses & 3 Mules. 1 Horse & 3 Mules belonging 61st Division, attended other duties	G.W.B.
"	24/7/16		Attended duties of Section, Inis & Horse Dip.	G.W.B.
"	25/7/16		Attended duties of Section, Inis, & Horse Dip. Cleared up & improved Billets.	G.W.B.
"	26/7/16		Evacuated 5 Horses belonging to 61st Division. Attended duties of Section, Inis & Dip.	G.W.B.

Army Form C. 2118.

WAR DIARY
or
INTELLIGENCE SUMMARY.
(Erase heading not required.)

Place	Date	Hour	Summary of Events and Information	Remarks and references to Appendices
ARRAS - S⁺ POL	27th		Attended to duties of Section Unit. Horse disp. Mare new Pharmacy.	G.W.B.
"	28th		Attended to duties of Section Unit. Horse disp. Repairing Roofs stables.	G.W.B.
"	29th		Attended duties of Section & both Horse disp. 5 Horses & 1 Mule to 4 M. Transferred to 61st Division. 3 Horses belonging to 61st Division. Packs up + cleaned to hcb. preparatory to moving. Received over XVII Corps Horse Dis to It Col Lah A.D.V.S.	G.W.B.
BEAULENCOURT	30th		Horse Section to F. Camp BEAULENCOURT.	G.W.B.

G.W. Bourne
Capt A.V.C

WAR DIARY
or
INTELLIGENCE SUMMARY.

Army Form C. 2118.

Place	Date	Hour	Summary of Events and Information	Remarks and references to Appendices
BEAULENCOURT	1/12/17		Attended duties of Section & awaited Orders	G.W.B
ETRICOURT	2/12/17		Moved Section to ETRICOURT & took over Billets from 2/1 North Midland M.V.S.	G.W.B.
"	3/12/17		Attended duties of Section, took over 307 Lab Gradle chin Co. & 315 Lab Construction Co.	G.W.B.
"	4/12/17		Attended duties of Section, visited D. B. & C Squadrons Northumberland Hussars, Evacuated 1 Horse sick for 59th Division M.V.S.	G.W.B.
"	5/12/17		Evacuated 9 Horses & 2 Mules, 3 Horses & 1 Mule belonging to 61st Division, attended other duties of Section, visited all units 182 Brigade Group, took over No 9 Section III Army Horse shop Co & visited.	G.W.B
"	6/12/17		Evacuated 6 Horses & 3 Mules 3 Horses & 3 Mules belonging to 61st Division, attended other duties of Section & units, & various visited 2/1 Field Ambulance	G.W.B.
"	7/12/17		Evacuated 6 Horses & 1 Mule, 1 Horse & 1 Mule belonging to 61st Division, attended other work of Section Units	G.W.B.
"	8/12/17		Attended work of Section & Units.	G.W.B.
"	9/12/17		Evacuated 4 Horses & 2 Mules, 1 Horse & 1 Mule belonging to 61st Division. Attended other work of Section Units.	G.W.B
"	10/12/17		Attended to duties of Section & other Units	G.W.B.

Army Form C. 2118.

WAR DIARY
or
INTELLIGENCE SUMMARY.
(Erase heading not required.)

Instructions regarding War Diaries and Intelligence Summaries are contained in F. S. Regs., Part II. and the Staff Manual respectively. Title pages will be prepared in manuscript.

Place	Date	Hour	Summary of Events and Information	Remarks and references to Appendices
ETRICOURT	10/12/17		Evacuated 6 Horses & 5 Mules, 2 Horses & 3 Mules belonging to 61st Division, attached to this Section to the Unit.	G.W.B
"	12/12/17		Evacuated 6 Horses & 3 Mules, 2 Horses belonging to 61st Division, attached other work of Section to Unit.	G.W.B
"	13/12/17		Evacuated 10 Horses & 2 Mules, 1 Mule belonging to 61st Division, attended other work of Section to Unit.	G.W.B.
"	14/12/17		Evacuated 5 Horses other than 61st Division, attended to other work of Section & Unit.	G.W.B.
"	15/12/17		Evacuated 5 Horses, 4 Horses belonging to 61st Division, attended other work of Unit & Section	G.W.B.
"	16/12/17		Evacuated 22 Horses & 2 Mules, 1 Horse & 1 Mule belonging to 61st Division, attended other work of Unit & Section	G.W.B.
"	17/12/17		Attended to work of Section to the Unit	G.W.B
"	18/12/17		Evacuated 5 Horses, 4 Horses belonging to 61st Division, attended other work of Section & Unit.	G.W.B
"	19/12/17		Chasses to duties of Section & the Unit, took over in addition 19th Reserve Park, 2nd Traffic Control Sqdrt, 173 Lab Co, 757 Lab Co.	G.W.B
"	20/12/17		Evacuated 12 Horses 6 belonging to 61st Division, attended other work of Section & Unit.	G.W.B

Army Form C. 2118.

WAR DIARY
or
INTELLIGENCE SUMMARY.
(Erase heading not required.)

Instructions regarding War Diaries and Intelligence Summaries are contained in F. S. Regs., Part II. and the Staff Manual respectively. Title pages will be prepared in manuscript.

Place	Date	Hour	Summary of Events and Information	Remarks and references to Appendices
ETRICOURT.	21/7/17		Attached 6 horses of Section to the Units.	G.W.B.
"	22/7/17		Attended to duties of Units Section	G.W.B
"	23/7/17		Evacuated 4 Horses belonging to 61st Division, attended to other duties of Section & Unit. Packed up preparatory to moving.	G.W.B.
CLERY.	24/7/17		Moved Section to CLERY.	G.W.B.
ETENEHEM.	25/7/17		Moved Section to ETENEHEM.	G.W.B.
"	26/7/17		Cleaned out & settled in Billets, visited outlying Section with D.A.D.V.S & attended to other work of Section	G.W.B
"	27/7/17		Attended to duties of Section, attended D.V.Q.	G.W.B.
"	28/7/17		Evacuated 1 Horse other than 61st Division visited Units at CERISSY, SAILLY LAURETTE, SAILLY-LE-SEC & VAUX & attended to duties of Section	G.W.B.
"	29/7/17		Attended to duties of Section, visited Units at MORCOURT & CHIPILLY.	G.W.B.
"	30/7/17		Attended to duties of Section, proceeded HARBONNIERES to billet Section	G.W.B.
HARBONNIERES	31/7/17		Moved Section to HARBONNIERES, Cleaned out Billets.	G.W.B.

G.W. Blossome
Capt A.V.C

WAR DIARY
or
INTELLIGENCE SUMMARY.
(Erase heading not required.)

Army Form C. 2118.

9 M/B Feby Jal 21

Place	Date	Hour	Summary of Events and Information	Remarks and references to Appendices
HARBONNIERES	1/8		Attached duties of Section & Units Cleaned up Billets.	G.W.B.
"	2/8		Attached duties of Section Chiefs. Visited Units at Le Quesnel	G.W.B.
"	3/8		Attached to duties of Section Chiefs.	G.W.B.
"	4/8		Evacuated 10 Horses & 1 Mule belonging 61st Division & 1 Mule other Ranks 61st Division.	G.W.B.
"	5/8		Attached to duties of Section Chiefs. Visited LEQUESNEL, RODOY, MARQUESTE, ARMUERES, BEAUCOURT.	G.W.B.
"	6/8		Attached to duties of Section Chiefs. Packed up ready for moving out.	G.W.B.
NESLE	7/8		Moved Section to NESLE	G.W.B.
"	8/8		Cleaned out Billets. Attached to duties of Section & visited Units.	G.W.B.
"	9/8		Attached to work of Section.	G.W.B.
"	10/8		Attached duties of Section. Visited DOUILLY. Found Suitable location for Section.	G.W.B.
DOUILLY	11/8		Visited FORESTE. Made final Suitable location. Moved Section to DOUILLY	G.W.B.
"	12/8		Distributed Stabling. Went a France party.	G.W.B.
"	13/8		Attached duties of Section. Started work of cleaning up Billets.	G.W.B.
"			Attached duties of Section. Visited FORESTE & arranged re Evacuation of horses.	G.W.B.
"			Carrying cleaning up & improving Billets.	G.W.B.
"	14/8		Attached duties of Section & Units. Commenced building lean to shed for O.C.	G.W.B.

WAR DIARY or INTELLIGENCE SUMMARY.

Army Form C. 2118.

Place	Date	Hour	Summary of Events and Information	Remarks and references to Appendices
DOUILLY	15th		Evacuated 30 Horses & 4 Mules, 16 Horses & 4 Mules belonging 61st Division (Drake) & 1 horse evacuated	G.W.B.
"	16th		2 belonging French Army) attended other duties of Section & building of Hut Carrison.	G.W.B.
"	17th		Attended duties of Section & Unit & carried on with building of Hut.	G.W.B.
"	18th		Attended duties of Section & Unit, carried on with improvement of Billets & building of Hut. Evacuated 12 Horses & 2 Mules belonging to 61st Division, attended other duties of Section & Unit. Completed hut for O.C. stored in.	G.W.B.
"	19th		Attended to work of Section & Unit. Commenced construction of Oven for Cookhouse, took remainder of personnel for Miss examination & classification	G.W.B.
"	20th		Attended to duties of Section & Unit & cleaned up Billets & improved surroundings.	G.W.B.
"	21st		Attended to duties of Section & Unit, lost on O/S/L/d A.T. 284 Co. R.E. at CROX-MOLIGNAUX, lost no. d mobilies 267 M.G.C. at FORESTE; cleaned up Billets.	G.W.B.
"	22nd		Evacuated 42 Horses & 4 Mules, 22 Horses & 4 Mules belonging to 61st Division	G.W.B.
"	23rd		Attended to duties of Section & Unit, proceeded with draining of yard & laying brick rubble.	G.W.B.
"	24th		Attended to duties of Section & Unit, laid brick rubble & proceeded with building Cookhouse for O.C.	G.W.B.

Army Form C. 2118.

WAR DIARY
or
INTELLIGENCE SUMMARY.
(Erase heading not required.)

Place	Date	Hour	Summary of Events and Information	Remarks and references to Appendices
DOUILLY.	25th		Evacuated 18 Horses & 2 Mules, 16 Horses & 2 Mules belonging to 61st Division, attended other duties of Section & Unit.	
"	26th		Attended to duties of Section & Unit, laid brick rattle yard & cleaned part of old straw	G.W.B.
"	27th		Attended to duties of Section & Unit, laid brick rattle yard & cleaned remainder of old straw	G.W.B.
"	28th		Attended to duties of Section & Unit, finished preparing S.T.s for Men's hut & pant horse	G.W.B.
"	29th		Evacuated 14 Horses, 4 Horses belonging to 61st Division, laid rubble in yard & attended other duties of Section & Unit.	G.W.B.
"	30th		Attended to duties of Section & Unit, Collected & started up Manure Dump.	G.W.B.
"	31st		Attended to duties of Section & Unit, attended Conference of D.A.D.V.S. Proceeded on 14 days leave to England.	G.W.B.

G.W. Bloxam
Capt. A.V.C.
Commanding 61st Mob Vet Sec

WAR DIARY
or
INTELLIGENCE SUMMARY.
(Erase heading not required.)

Army Form C. 2118.

61D Mot- Vety Sec

Vol 2

Place	Date	Hour	Summary of Events and Information	Remarks and references to Appendices
DOUILLY	1/2/18		Evacuated 2.6 Horses & 7 Mules. 1 Horse & 2 Mules to 61st Div.	JMR
DOUILLY	2/2/18		" att⁴ to duties of Section	JMR
"	3/2/18		ditto	JMR
"	4/2/18		ditto	JMR
"	5/2/18		Evacuated 21 Horses & 10 Mules. 12 Horses & 3 Mules 61st Div.	JMR
"	6/2/18		" att⁴ to duties of Section	JMR
"	7/2/18		ditto	JMR
"	8/2/18		Evacuated 4.8 Horses. 3 Horses 61st Div. 1 att⁴ to duties of Section	JMR
"	9/2/18		" att⁴ to duties of Section	JMR
"	10/2/18		ditto	JMR
"	11/2/18		ditto	JMR
"	12/2/18		Evacuated 3.3 Horses & 3 Mules. 8 Horses & 1 mule 61st Div.	JMR
"	13/2/18		" att⁴ to duties of Section	JMR

Army Form C. 2118.

WAR DIARY
or
INTELLIGENCE SUMMARY.
(Erase heading not required.)

Instructions regarding War Diaries and Intelligence Summaries are contained in F. S. Regs., Part II. and the Staff Manual respectively. Title pages will be prepared in manuscript.

Place	Date	Hour	Summary of Events and Information	Remarks and references to Appendices
Dewlly	13/2/18		Attd to duties of Section	ditto
"	14/2/18		ditto	ditto
"	15/2/18		Evacuated 33 Horses & 1 Mule, 5 Horses 61st Div	ditto
"	16/2/18		Attd to duties of Section	ditto
"	17/2/18		ditto	ditto
"	18/2/18		ditto & handed over to Capt Nicome A.V.C.	ditto
			[signature] Lieut AVC	
"	19/2/18		Returned from leave took over from Lieut Proctor A.V.C.	G.W.B.
"	19/2/18		Evacuated 19 Horses & 1 Mule, 7 Horses belonging to 61st Division Picketed which rations & other duties of Section	G.W.B.
"	20/2/18		Attended duties of Section Picket	G.W.B.
"	21/2/18		Attended duties of Section Picket & attended Conference at D.A.D.V.S.'s Office	G.W.B.
"	22/2/18		Attended duties of Section & Picket Evacuated 3 Horses & 1 Mule, 6 Horses belonging to 61st Division	G.W.B.

WAR DIARY
or
INTELLIGENCE SUMMARY.
(Erase heading not required.)

Army Form C. 2118.

Place	Date	Hour	Summary of Events and Information	Remarks and references to Appendices
DOUILLY.	23/8		Attached to duties of Section Unit, proceed to dig garden (1/2 acre) & prepare for cultivation of same.	G.M.B.
"	24/8		Attached to duties of Section Unit. Carried on with preparation of garden.	G.M.B
"	25/8		Attached to duties of Section Unit - garden cultivation	G.M.B
"	26/8		Evacuated 13 horses & 4 Mules & 1 Horse & 2 Mules belonging to 61st Division	G.M.B
"	27/8		Attached to duties of Section Unit - Agriculture.	G.M.B.
"	28/8		Attached to duties of Section Unit. Attended Conference D.A.D.V.S., planted various seeds in garden	G.M.B

G.M.Blossom
Capt. A.V.C

26

61 Mob Vety Sec A.D.

WAR DIARY
or
INTELLIGENCE SUMMARY.

Army Form C. 2118.
Vol 23

Place	Date	Hour	Summary of Events and Information	Remarks and references to Appendices
DOUILLY	1/3/15		Evacuated 9 Horses & 3 Mules, 4 Horses & 2 Mules to hospital of 61st Division. Attended other duties of Section Units.	G.W.B.
"	2/3/15		Attended most of Section's disabled units, carried on with preparation of Garden.	G.W.B.
"	3/3/15		Attended duties of Section Unit. Garden.	G.W.B
"	4/3/15		Attended duties of Section Unit.	G.W.B
"	5/3/15		Evacuated 24 Horses & 3 Mules. 1 Horse & 2 Mules belonging to 61st Division	G.W.B
"	6/3/15		Attended the Duties of Section Unit. Attended duties of Section Unit, Selected site for advanced Aid Post at VINEVEQUE & mapped out route for Cases.	G.W.B
"	7/3/15		Attended Duties of Section Unit. Cultivation of Garden.	G.W.B
"	8/3/15		Evacuated 11 Horses, 5 Horses belonging to 61st Division, attended other duties of Section Unit.	G.W.B.
"	9/3/15		Attended Duties of Section Unit & Cultivation of garden, complied with order as to Summer Time at 11 p.m.	G.W.B.
"	10/3/17		Attended to duties of Section Unit.	G.W.B.
"	11/3/17		Attended to duties of Section Unit, Cultivation of Garden.	G.W.B.

Army Form C. 2118.

WAR DIARY
or
INTELLIGENCE SUMMARY.
(Erase heading not required.)

Instructions regarding War Diaries and Intelligence Summaries are contained in F. S. Regs., Part II. and the Staff Manual respectively. Title pages will be prepared in manuscript.

Place	Date	Hour	Summary of Events and Information	Remarks and references to Appendices
DOUILLY.	12/3/18		Evacuated 32 Horses, all other than 61st Division, attached to the duties Section Unit, Carried on till Easter week.	G.W.B.
"	13/3/18		Attended to duties of Section & Unit, prepared for inspection by D.A.D.V.S & slept to until Warned 5.30 P.M. not coming.	G.W.B.
"	14/3/18		Attended to duties of Section & Unit, took over from D.A.D.V.S proceeding on leave	G.W.B.
"	15/3/18		Evacuated 8 Horses & 4 Mules, 6 Horses & 2 Mules belonging to 61st Division. Attended to the duties of Section Unit, & D.A.D.V.S.	G.W.B.
"	16/3/18		Attended to duties of Section Unit, & D.A.D.V.S.	G.W.B.
"	17/3/18		Attended to duties of Section, Unit, & D.A.D.V.S.	G.W.B.
"	18/3/18		Attended to duties of Section, Unit, & D.A.D.V.S.	G.W.B.
"	19/3/18		Evacuated 26 Horses & 6 Mules, 7 Horses belonging to 61st Division, attended to the duties of Section, Unit, & D.A.D.V.S.	G.W.B.
"	20/3/18		Attended to duties of Section, visited Unit, attended duties of D.A.D.V.S.	G.W.B.
"	21/3/18		Attended to duties of Section, & D.A.D.V.S, complied with instruction re manning Battle Zone, fell out and at Pat VILLEVEQUE until dawn at night owing to heavy shelling, Evacuated 24 Horses	G.W.B.

Army Form C. 2118.

WAR DIARY
or
INTELLIGENCE SUMMARY.
(Erase heading not required.)

Place	Date	Hour	Summary of Events and Information	Remarks and references to Appendices
DOUILLY	21/3/18		and 3 Mules to V.C.C.S. HAM. 13 Horses & 1 Mule belonging to 61st Division. ~~Sections to Billancourt~~	G.W.B.
BILLANCOURT	22/3/18		Moved Section & 13 Wounded to BILLANCOURT, Withdrew men from close V.C.C.S.11 AM.	G.W.B.
{LIANCOURT VILLERS-LE-ROYE	23/3/18		Evacuated 9 Horses & Mules from NESLE, 2 Horses & 3 Mules belonging to 61st Division, moved Section to LIANCOURT, moved Section to VILLERS-LE-ROYE	G.W.B. G.W.B.
{LIANCOURT DAMERY	24/3/18		Moved Section to LIANCOURT, moved Section to DAMERY.	G.W.B.
DAMERY	25/3/18		Moved Section to ARVILLERS.	G.W.B.
GUYENCOURT	26/3/18		Moved Section & travelled to GUYENCOURT.	G.W.B.
"	27/3/18		Attended Returns of Section, visited A.D.M.S. & found 2/2 F.A. attended to Sick of D.A.D.V.S.	G.W.B.
DOMMARTIN	28/3/18		Moved Section to DOMMARTIN, picked Stragglers took in one to hosp.	G.W.B.
SAINS	29/3/18		Moved Section to SAINS, visited D.H.Q. attended to duties of D.A.D.V.S.	G.W.B.
"	30/3/18		Attended to duties of Section, visited Units at COTTENCHY.	G.W.B.
SALOUEL	31/3/18		Moved Section & Sick animals to SALOUEL, attended duties of D.A.D.V.S.	G.W.B.

G.W. Blaine
Capt. A.V.C.

WAR DIARY or INTELLIGENCE SUMMARY

Army Form C. 2118.

61 Mot Vety See Vol 24

Place	Date	Hour	Summary of Events and Information	Remarks and references to Appendices
SALOUEL	1/7/18		Evacuated to V.C.C.5 PICQUIGNY 7 Horses 3 belonging to 61st Division. Visited D.H.Q attached to Hd Qrs of D.A.D.V.S. transferred on to D.A.D.V.S.	G.W.B
"	2/7/18		Evacuated 16 Horses & 2 Mules to V.C.C.5. 11 Horses belonging to 61st Division visited 182 B'de & 6th M.G. Battalion	G.W.B
"	3/7/18		Evacuated 14 Horses & 3 Mules 4 Horses & 3 Mules belonging to 61st Division attended other duties of Section & Units	G.W.B
"	4/7/18		Attend D.A.D.V.S's Conference D.H.Q PISSY. Sent Corpse Prink to cut switch location M.V.S at SAISSEVAL. attended other duties of Sections & Units	G.W.B
"	5/7/18		Visited proposed location SAISSEVAL. Visited D.H.Q. PISSY. attended duties of Section	G.W.B
"	6/7/18		Attend duties of Section & Units	G.W.B
CLAIRY	7/7/18		Moved Section to CLAIRY.	G.W.B
ARGUEL	8/7/18		Moved Section to ARGUEL. Evacuated 4 Horses to PICQUIGNY	G.W.B
"	9/7/18		Attend to duties of Section, erected Bivouacs & took in 69 Animals.	G.W.B
"	10/7/18		Evacuated 4 & 3 Horses & 13 Mules 12 Horses & Mules belonging to 61st Division	G.W.B
"	11/7/18		Attend to duties of Section visited XIX Corps MOLLIENS-Vidame & arranged with Staff Captain for Forage Rations & method of rejoining Division.	G.W.B

WAR DIARY
or
INTELLIGENCE SUMMARY.
(Erase heading not required.)

Army Form C. 2118.

Instructions regarding War Diaries and Intelligence Summaries are contained in F. S. Regs., Part II. and the Staff Manual respectively. Title pages will be prepared in manuscript.

Place	Date	Hour	Summary of Events and Information	Remarks and references to Appendices
ARGUEL	12/7/8		Evacuated 4 Horses & 3 Mules, 1 Horse belonging to 61st Division by road to ABBEVILLE	G.W.B.
"			Moved Section to ABBEVILLE	G.W.B.
ABBEYILLE	13/7/8		Moved Section to Ste AUSTREBERTHE	G.W.B.
Ste AUSTREBERTHE	14/7/8		Moved Section to PETIT ST POL (FRUGES)	G.W.B.
PETIT ST POL (FRUGES)	15/7/8		Moved Section to LAMBRES, reported to D.A.D.V.S. on rejoining Division	G.W.B.
LAMBRES	16/7/8		Attended to duties of Section, cleaning up of Billets	G.W.B.
"	17/7/8		Evacuated 4 Horses & 1 Mule, 3 Horses & 1 Mule belonging to 61st Division, attached other duties of Section Work.	G.W.B.
"	18/7/8		Attended duties of Section. Conference of D.A.D.V.S. + Court of Inquiry re Pte Hargreaves.	G.W.B.
"	19/7/8		Attended duties of Section, visited units. Evacuated 1 Horse & 1 Mule, 1 Horse belonging to 61st Division	G.W.B.
"	20/7/8		Evacuated 1 Horse & 3 Mules, 3 Mules belonging to 61st Division, attended to duties of Section	G.W.B.
"	21/7/8		Evacuated 2 Horses belonging to 61st Division, visited units, attended other duties	G.W.B.
"	22/7/8		Attended to duties of Section Work	G.W.B.
"	23/7/8		Visited units & civil patrols, attended to duties of Section.	G.W.B.
"	24/7/8		Evacuated 3 Mules, 2 belonging to 61st Division, attended to the duties of Section	G.W.B.
"	25/7/8		Evacuated 2 Horses belonging to 61st Division, attended duties of work	G.W.B.

Army Form C. 2118.

WAR DIARY
or
INTELLIGENCE SUMMARY.
(Erase heading not required.)

Instructions regarding War Diaries and Intelligence Summaries are contained in F. S. Regs., Part II. and the Staff Manual respectively. Title pages will be prepared in manuscript.

Place	Date	Hour	Summary of Events and Information	Remarks and references to Appendices
LAMBRES.	26/7/18		Attnd A.D.V.S X I Corps. D.A.D.V.S 61st Division on inspection of 182 Inf B'de, attended to the duties of section O.i.k.	G.W.B
"	27/7/18		Evacuated 0 additions + 1 Mule, 1 Horse belonging to 61st Division, visited Units r.c.	G.W.B.
"	28/7/18		Evacuated 4 Horses + 1 Mule belonging to 61st Division, attended other duties + visited Unit.	G.W.B
"	29/7/18		Evacuated 2 Horses + 1 Mule, belonging to 61st Division, visited Units + attended other duties.	G.W.B
"	30/7/18		Evacuated 5 Horses, 3 belonging to 61st Division, visited Units + attended other duties.	G.W.B

G.W. Beaone
Capt A.V.C.

Army Form C. 2118.

WAR DIARY
or
INTELLIGENCE SUMMARY.
(Erase heading not required.)

M.V.S. No 2

Place	Date	Hour	Summary of Events and Information	Remarks and references to Appendices
LAMBRES	1/5/18		Evacuated 15 Horses & 1 Mule, 13 Horses belonging to 61st Division, attended other duties of Section and visited Units.	G.W.B
"	2/5/18		Evacuated 1 Horse belonging to 61st Division, attended duties of Section and visited Units.	G.W.B
"	3/5/18		Attended Duties of Section and visited Units.	G.W.B
"	4/5/18		Attended Duties of Section and visited Units.	G.W.B
"	5/5/18		Attended Duties of Section and visited Units.	G.W.B
"	6/5/18		Evacuated 4 Horses, 3 Horses belonging to 61st Division, attended Field General Court Martial at AIRE on Pte Haines to 61st Division, attended other	G.W.B
"	7/5/18		Evacuated 7 Horses, 1 Horse belonging to 61st Division, attended other duties, visited Units, promulgated Sentence of 2 years I.H.L on Pte Steward A.V.C	G.W.B
"	8/5/18		Attended duties of Unit & Section, visited M.G. Battalion.	G.W.B
"	9/5/18		Evacuated 1 Horse & 2 Mules, all other than 61st Division, visited Units & attended other Duties of Section	G.W.B
"	10/5/18		Evacuated 3 Horses all other than 61st Division visited Units & attended other Duties of Section, 10 Horses present, owing to Units not receiving Orders sufficiently early.	G.W.B

Army Form C. 2118.

WAR DIARY
or
INTELLIGENCE SUMMARY.
(Erase heading not required.)

Instructions regarding War Diaries and Intelligence Summaries are contained in F. S. Regs., Part II. and the Staff Manual respectively. Title pages will be prepared in manuscript.

Place	Date	Hour	Summary of Events and Information	Remarks and references to Appendices
LAMBRES.	11/5/18		Evacuated 4 horses, 2 horses belonging to 61st Division, visited units & attended other duties of Section	G.W.B.
"	12/5/18		Attended to duties of Section, visited units	G.W.B.
"	13/5/18		Evacuated 9 horses & 2 mules, 1 Horse belonging to 61st Division, visited units	G.W.B.
"	14/5/18		Evacuated 4 horses, 1 Horse belonging to 61st Division, visited units & attended other duties of Section	G.W.B.
"	15/5/18		Evacuated 3 horses & 3 Mules, all other than 61st Division, attended both duties of Section, visited units & Civilians.	G.W.B
"	16/5/18		Attended to both of Sections, visited units.	G.W.B
"	17/5/18		Evacuated 3 horses, 1 horse belonging to 61st Division, attended other duties of Section, visited units & Civilians, commenced digging bomb shelter	G.W.B
"	18/5/18		Evacuated 1 horse & 1 Mule, other than 61st Division, attended other duties of Section, visited units & Civilians, proceeded with Bomb Shelter.	G.W.B.
"	19/5/18		Attended duties of Section, visited units & Civilians, completed with Bomb shelter.	G.W.B.
"	20/5/18			G.W.B.

WAR DIARY
or
INTELLIGENCE SUMMARY.

(Erase heading not required.)

Army Form C. 2118.

Instructions regarding War Diaries and Intelligence Summaries are contained in F. S. Regs., Part II. and the Staff Manual respectively. Title pages will be prepared in manuscript.

Place	Date	Hour	Summary of Events and Information	Remarks and references to Appendices
LAMBRES	20/5/18		Attended duties of Section. Visited Units & Civilian Cases.	G.W.B.
"	21/5/18		Attended duties of Section. Visited units. Improved Board sheets	G.W.B.
"	22/5/18		Evacuated 14 Horses & 3 Mules, 4 Horses & 1 Mule belonging to 61st Division attached. Other duties of Section. Visited Units.	G.W.B.
"	23/5/18		Evacuated 1 Horse & other than 61st Division, attended duties of Section, visited Units & Civilian Cases.	G.W.B.
"	24/5/18		Evacuated 6 Horses, 3 Horses belonging to 61st Division & other duties of Section.	G.W.B.
"	25/5/18		Other duties of Section. Attended duties of Section. Visited Units. Visited Civilians.	G.W.B. G.W.B.
"	26/5/18		Evacuated 3 Horses & 3 Mules, 1 Horse & 1 Mule belonging to 61st Division. Visited Units.	G.W.B.
"	27/5/18		Attended to duties of Section & Units, 6 K.R. War Regt. Transport Lines stables 13 mules & 1 Horse sick.	G.W.B.
"	28/5/18		Evacuated 1 Mule other than 61st Division attended other duties of Section, visited Units & Civilians.	G.W.B.
"	29/5/18		Evacuated 16 Horses & 2 Mules; 10 Horses & 2 Mules belonging to 61st Division, attended other duties of Section, visited Units & Civilians.	G.W.B.

Army Form C. 2118.

WAR DIARY
or
INTELLIGENCE SUMMARY.
(Erase heading not required.)

Instructions regarding War Diaries and Intelligence Summaries are contained in F. S. Regs., Part II. and the Staff Manual respectively. Title pages will be prepared in manuscript.

Place	Date	Hour	Summary of Events and Information	Remarks and references to Appendices
LAMBRES	30/5/16		Evacuated 8 Horses & 3 Mules, 6 Horses belonging to 61st Division afflicted other station of Section visited units.	G.W.B.
"	31/5/16		Attended duties of Section & visited units.	G.W.B.

G.W. Blossom
Capt. A.V.C.
Commanding 61st Mob Vet Sec.

WAR DIARY or INTELLIGENCE SUMMARY

Army Form C. 2118.

61st Res. Vet. Sect.

Vol 26

Place	Date	Hour	Summary of Events and Information	Remarks and references to Appendices
LAMBRES	1/6/18		Evacuated 4 Horses & 2 Mules, 2 Horses belonging to 61st Division, attended to duties of Section, visited trails.	G.W.B.
"	2/6/18		Evacuated 7 Horses & 4 Mules, 1 Horse & 2 Mules belonging to 61st Division, attended to duties of Section, visited trails & Civilian cases.	G.W.B.
"	3/6/18		S. Sergt Roach transferred to No 5 Vet. Hospital, attended duties of Section, visited trails & Civilian cases.	G.W.B.
"	4/6/18		Evacuated 2 Horses & 1 Mule, 1 Horse & 1 Mule belonging to 61st Division, attended other duties of Section, visited trails & Civilian cases.	G.W.B.
"	5/6/18		Evacuated 6 Horses & 1 Mule other than 61st Division, attended duties of Section, visited trails.	G.W.B.
"	6/6/18		Evacuated 5 Horses & 2 Mules, 1 Horse & 2 Mules belonging to 61st Division, attended other work of Section, visited trails & Civilians.	G.W.B.
"	7/6/18		Evacuated 1 Horse & 1 Mule, 1 Mule belonging to 61st Division, attended other duties of Section, visited trails & Civilian cases.	G.W.B.
"	8/6/18		Evacuated 1 Horse & 1 Mule, other than 61st Division, visited trails & attended other duties of Section.	G.W.B.
"	9/6/18		Evacuated 3 Horses other than 61st Division attended duties of Section, visited trails.	G.W.B.
"	10/6/18		Evacuated 6 Horses & 4 Horses belonging to 61st Division, attended other duties of Section & visited trails.	G.W.B.

WAR DIARY
or
INTELLIGENCE SUMMARY.

(Erase heading not required.)

Army Form C. 2118.

1901 War Vet Seen

Instructions regarding War Diaries and Intelligence Summaries are contained in F. S. Regs. Part II. and the Staff Manual respectively. Title pages will be prepared in manuscript.

Place	Date	Hour	Summary of Events and Information	Remarks and references to Appendices
LANDRES	20/6		Attended duties of section, visited units	G.W.B
"	21/6		Evacuated 3 Mules, 1 Mule belonging to 61st Division, attached other Mules of section, visited units	G.W.B
"	22/6		Evacuated 3 Horses & 1 Mule other than 61st Division, attached duties of section & units	G.W.B
"	23/6		Visited calls, (Civilian Cases)	G.W.B
"	24/6		Evacuated 2 Horses & 1 Mule, 3 Horses & 1 Mule belonging to 61st Division attached other	G.W.B
"			Duties & visited units	G.W.B
"	25/6		Evacuated 5 Horses & 4 Horses belonging to 61st Division, attached other duties & visited units	G.W.B
"			Visited units (Civilian Cases)	G.W.B
"	26/6		Evacuated 5 Horses belonging to 61st Division, attached other than (Civilian Cases)	G.W.B
"	27/6		Evacuated 4 Horses other than 61st Division, visited units (Civilian Cases)	G.W.B
"	28/6		Evacuated 2 Horses & 1 Mule other than 61st Division, attached other duties of section & visited units (Civilian Cases)	G.W.B
"	29/6		Evacuated 2 Horses belonging to 61st Division attached other duties & visited units	G.W.B
"			Evacuated 3 Horses, 1 Horse belonging to 61st Division, visited units (Civilian Cases)	G.W.B
"	30/6		Evacuated 2 Horses & 1 Mule, 2 Horses belonging to 61st Division, visited units & attended other duties	G.W.B

G.W. Beveau Capt. V.C.

Army Form C. 2118.

WAR DIARY
or
INTELLIGENCE SUMMARY.
(Erase heading not required.)

Oct Nos. 121 - Ens

Instructions regarding War Diaries and Intelligence Summaries are contained in F. S. Regs. Part II. and the Staff Manual respectively. Title pages will be prepared in manuscript.

Place	Date	Hour	Summary of Events and Information	Remarks and references to Appendices
LAMBRES	11/6/18		Evacuated 4 Horses + 3 Mules to XI V.E.5, 2 Horses + 3 Mules belonging to 61st Division. Evacuated 2 Mules + 1 Horse other than 61st Division to Remount Depot NOYELLES, attended to the duties of Section + visited Units.	P.W.B.
"	12/6/18		Evacuated 1 Horse + 3 Mules, 2 Mules belonging to 61st Division, attended to the duties of Section and visited Units.	G.W.B.
"	13/6/18		Attended duties of Section, Visited Units + Civilian Cases.	G.W.B.
"	14/6/18		Evacuated 8 Horses, 4 Horses belonging to 61st Division, also 3 other Ranks, visited Units.	G.W.B.
"			Ordered 2 Horses to Pothepone M.V.S. THEROUANNE.	G.W.B.
"	15/6/18		Evacuated 1 Horse + 1 Mule other Ranks 61st Division, attended to duties of Section visited Units	G.W.B.
"	16/6/18		Evacuated 2 Horses + 2 Mules, 1 Mule belonging 61st Division, attended to the duties of Section, Visited Units + Civilian Cases.	G.W.B.
"	17/6/18		Evacuated 5 Horses + 1 Mule, 2 Horses + 1 Mule belonging 61st Division, attended Remount Lands, to the duties of Section, Visited Units + Civilian Cases.	G.W.B.
"	18/6/18		Evacuated 6 Horses + 4 Mules, 3 Horses + 3 Mules belonging to 61st Division, attended Otter, took of Section, Visited Units.	G.W.B.
"	19/6/18		Attended duties of Section, Units, Visited Units + Civilian Cases.	G.W.B.

WAR DIARY
or
INTELLIGENCE SUMMARY.
(Erase heading not required.)

Army Form C. 2118.

61st M.V.S. Vol 27

Place	Date	Hour	Summary of Events and Information	Remarks and references to Appendices
LAMBRES	1/7/18		Evacuated 8 Horses & 2 Mules 6 Horses & 1 Mule belonging to 61st Division.	G.W.B.
"	2/7/18		Attended duties of Section. Visited hosp. & Civilian Cases	G.W.B.
"	3/7/18		Evacuated 3 Horses & 1 Mule. 1 Horse belonging to 61st Division. Attended other duties Visited kraals	G.W.B.
"	4/7/18		Evacuated 13 Horses & 5 Horses belonging to 61st Division attended other duties	G.W.B.
"	5/7/18		Attended to duties of Section. visited kraals & Civilian Cases	G.W.B.
"	6/7/18		Evacuated 8 Horses other than 61st Division, Visited kraals & Civilian Cases.	G.W.B.
"			Evacuated 9 Horses & 1 Mule, 3 Horses & 1 Mule belonging to 61st Division, attended other duties. Visited kraals & Civilian Cases.	G.W.B.
"	7/7/18		1 Horse belonging to 61st Division Patcheed (foot) attended duties of Section. Visited kraals & Civilian Cases.	G.W.B.
"	8/7/18		Evacuated 1 Horse belonging to 61st Division, attended other duties Visited kraals & Civilian Cases.	G.W.B.
"	9/7/18		Evacuated 4 Horses & 2 Mules, 3 Horses & 1 Mule belonging to 61st Division. Visited kraals & treated Civilian Cases	G.W.B.
"	10/7/18		Evacuated 2 Horses, 1 Horse belonging to 61st Division. Visited kraals & Civilian Cases, & attended other duties of Section	G.W.B.
"	11/7/18		Attended duties of Section Visited kraals	G.W.B.

Army Form C. 2118.

WAR DIARY
or
INTELLIGENCE SUMMARY.
(Erase heading not required.)

Instructions regarding War Diaries and Intelligence Summaries are contained in F. S. Regs., Part II. and the Staff Manual respectively. Title pages will be prepared in manuscript.

Place	Date	Hour	Summary of Events and Information	Remarks and references to Appendices
LAMBRES	12/7/15		Evacuated 2 Horses + 1 Mule, 1 Horse + 1 Mule belonging to 61st Division visited unit & Civilian Cases	G.W.B.
"	13/7/15		Evacuated 3 Horses belonging to 61st Division visited unit & Civilian Cases, attended Stables. A.T.R.E. 2.6.4 p.m.	G.W.B
"	14/7/15		Evacuated 3 Horses + 3 Mules, 1 Horse + 1 Mule belonging to 61st Division, visited Units & Civilian Cases	G.W.B.
"	15/7/15		Evacuated 5 Horses other than 61st Division attended other duties & visited units	G.W.B.
"	16/7/15		Evacuated 5 Horses + 1 Mule belonging to 61st Division, visited Unit (Civilian Cases)	G.W.B
"	17/7/15		Evacuated 1 Horse (Batchelor 109 pr.) belonging 61st Division visited units, attended other duties	G.W.B
"	18/7/15		Evacuated 1 Horse 61st Division, visited units & S.A.A.	G.W.B.
"	19/7/15		Evacuated 1 Horse other than 61st Division, Examined 17 Remounts for 61 M.G. Bn. visited unit & Civilian Cases & attended other duties.	G.W.B
"	20/7/15		Evacuated 1 Horse + 1 Mule other than 61st Division attended other duties & visited Civilian Cases.	G.W.B
"	21/7/15		Attended duties of Section visited Units & Civilian Cases.	G.W.B

Army Form C. 2118.

WAR DIARY
or
INTELLIGENCE SUMMARY.
(Erase heading not required.)

Instructions regarding War Diaries and Intelligence Summaries are contained in F. S. Regs., Part II. and the Staff Manual respectively. Title pages will be prepared in manuscript.

Place	Date	Hour	Summary of Events and Information	Remarks and references to Appendices
LES & WARDRECQUES	22/7/18		Evacuated 3 Horses & 2 Mules, 1 Horse & 1 Mule other than 61st Division (78 U.S.A. Div.) (Whole 61st Div. Entrained 100 Frs.) moved Section to WARDRECQUES.	App. B.
"	23/7/18		Change of Billet & that of Sick Corps attached to Section & Ration & Ambulance Cars. Refixed stations & civilian dog both ratios	App. B.
"	24/7/18		Attached to ratios of section & civilian cases	App. B.
"	25/7/18		Attached ratios of Section, visited their Civilian Cases.	App. B.
"	26/7/18		Evacuated 6 Horses to No 23 Vety Hospital STONER, attended ratios of Section & Civilian Cases	App. B.
"	27/7/18		Attached ratios of section, visited their	App. B.
"	28/7/18		Attached ratios of Section, visited Units	App. B.
"	29/7/18		Evacuated 4 Horses & 2 Mules, 2 Horses & 1 Mule belonging to 61st Division, visited Units	App. B.
"	30/7/18		Evacuated 4 Horses & 1 Mule, belonging to 61st Division, visited Units	App. B.
"	31/7/18		Attached to ratios of Section, visited Units, specialist ready for moving	App. B.

G.W. Bloxam
Capt. A.V.C.

WAR DIARY
or
INTELLIGENCE SUMMARY.

Army Form C. 2118.

6th Mob. Vety Sec
Vol 28

Place	Date	Hour	Summary of Events and Information	Remarks and references to Appendices
LAMBRES	1/6/18		Moved Section to LAMBRES. Closer to Battalions at Bittekfk.	G.M.B.
"	2/6/18		Attended to duties of Section, visited Units	G.M.B.
"	3/6/18		Attended to duties of Section visited Units. Civilian Cases.	G.M.B.
"	4/6/18		Attended to duties of Section visited Units. (Civilian Cases Evacuated 3 Horses, 2 Horses	G.M.B.
"	5/6/18		belonging 61st Division (Horse Ambulance 1st Division) Attended duties of Section. Visited Units, visited BOESIGHEM	G.M.B.
"	6/6/18		Attended duties of Section sent man BOESIGHEM teaming up fatigues.	G.M.B.
"	7/6/18		Attended duties of Section sent man BOESIGHEM to take over from 5th M.V.S.	G.M.B.
BOESIGHEM	8/6/18		Visited Civilian Cases, moved Section to BOESIGHEM, packed up & turned in parts Billets.	G.M.B.
"	9/6/18		Settled into Billets, attended to duties of Section, attended Conference D.A.D.V.S. & visited Units.	G.M.B.
			Evacuated 5 Horses + 4 Mules, 1 Horse belonging to 61st Division, attended other duties of	
			Section visited Units.	G.M.B.
"	10/6/18		Attended duties of Section visited Units, improved Billets.	G.M.B.
"	11/6/18		Attended duties of Section Evacuated 3 Horses & 2 Mules, 2 Mules belonging to 61st Division	G.M.B.
			visited Units.	
"	12/6/18		Evacuated 3 Horses + 1 Mule, 1 Horse belonging to 61st Division, attended other duties of Section	G.M.B.
			visited Units.	G.M.B.

Army Form C. 2118.

WAR DIARY
or
INTELLIGENCE SUMMARY.
(Erase heading not required.)

Place	Date	Hour	Summary of Events and Information	Remarks and references to Appendices
BOESINGHEM	13/5/18		Attended duties of Section, visited Units in the Area.	G.M.B.
"	14/5/18		Evacuated 4 Horses 3 belonging to 61st Division, visited Units, attended other duties of Section	G.M.B.
"	15/5/18		Attended to duties of Section & visited Units.	G.M.B.
"	16/5/18		Evacuated 4 Horses & 2 Mules, 3 Horses belonging to 61st Division visited Units & attended	G.M.B.
"	17/5/18		Other duties of Section	G.M.B.
"	18/5/18		Visited Units & attended duties of Section	G.M.B.
"	19/5/18		Visited Units & attended duties of Section. Evacuated 9 Horses & 2 Mules 3 Horses belonging 61st Div.	G.M.B.
"	20/5/18		Attended duties of Section & visited Units & Horses & Mules belonging to 1st Division	G.M.B.
"	21/5/18		Evacuated 9 Horses 1 belonging to 61st Division, visited Units & attended other duties	G.M.B.
"	22/5/18		Visited Units & attended duties of Section	G.M.B.
"			Evacuated 10 Horses & 2 Mules 6 of the Horses 61st Division, attended other duties &	G.M.B.
"			Visited Units, attended Another A.T.R.E.	G.M.B.
"	23/5/18		Attended duties of Section, visited Units & Anthrax Cases.	G.M.B.
"	24/5/18		Evacuated 9 Horses & 1 Mule, 4 Horses & 1 Mule belonging to 61st Div. visited Units & attended	G.M.B.
"			other duties, visited Anthrax Cases.	G.M.B.
"	25/5/18		Attended duties of Section visited Units & Anthrax Cases.	G.M.B.

Army Form C. 2118.

WAR DIARY
or
INTELLIGENCE SUMMARY.
(Erase heading not required.)

Instructions regarding War Diaries and Intelligence Summaries are contained in F. S. Regs., Part II and the Staff Manual respectively. Title pages will be prepared in manuscript.

Place	Date	Hour	Summary of Events and Information	Remarks and references to Appendices
BOESEGHEM	26/8		Evacuated 7 Horses, 1 Horse belonging to 61st Division, attended other duties of Section &	G.M.B.
"	27/8		distributed.	G.M.B.
"			Attended to duties of Section & Field Units & Civilian Cases.	
"	28/8		Evacuated 9 Horses & Mule, 2 Horses belonging to 61st Division, attended other duties & Section	G.M.B.
"			Units.	G.M.B.
"	29/8		Attended duties of Section & Field Units & Civilian Cases.	G.M.B.
"	30/8		Evacuated 3 Horses belonging to 61st Division Field Units, attended other duties	
"			& Mule & Civilian Cases.	
"	31/8		Evacuated 1 Mule belonging to 61st Division, Field Crew, Field Ambulances &	G.M.B.
"			also an D.A.D.V.S. looking for new location for Section.	

G.M. Blencowe
Capt. A.V.C.
A.D.V.S.

WAR DIARY or INTELLIGENCE SUMMARY

Army Form C. 2118.

61 Mob Vety Sec

Vol 29

Place	Date	Hour	Summary of Events and Information	Remarks and references to Appendices
BOESEGHEM	1/8		Attended duties of Section. Visited Units & Ambce Cases.	G.M.B.
TANNAY.	2/8		Moved Section to TANNAY. Attended to duties. Cleaned out Billets &c.	G.M.B.
"	3/8		Attended to duties of Section. Visited Units HAZEBROUCK & NEUF BERQUIN.	G.M.B.
"	4/8		Attended to duties of Section. Visited & selected site for new horse of Section	G.M.B.
ROUSSEL FARM	5/8		Moved Section to ROUSSEL FARM N.B.d.4.8. Cleaned out Billet & erected Shelter &c.	G.M.B.
"	6/8		Attended duties of Section. Cleaned up Billets, visited Units, attended Conference D.A.D.V.S.	G.M.B.
"	7/8		Attended duties of Section. Visited Sch.t & built other Huts	G.M.B.
"	8/8		Attended duties of Section. Inspected Billets, visited Units.	G.M.B.
"	9/8		Drew material for Cook house, horse lines forage Barn, attended Manoeuvres, Evacuated 1 horse belonging to 61st Division, & 2 horses other than 61st Division. G.D. v. 5XT Corps visited Section	G.M.B.
"	10/8		Attended duties of Section, foraged building material for Billet improvements, visited Units	G.M.B.
"	11/8		Attended duties of Section. Private hacking for Stables, filled up broken bath	G.M.B.
"	12/8		Attended duties of Section. Visited Units & Field Ambce.	G.M.B.
"	13/8		Attended duties of Section. Evacuated 3 horses & 2 Mules, all belonging to 61st Division	G.M.B.
"	14/8		Attended Conference of D.A.D.V.S. Handed over to Captain Proch R.V.C. & proceeded to U.K. on 14 days leave.	G.M.B.

Army Form C. 2118.

WAR DIARY
or
INTELLIGENCE SUMMARY.
(Erase heading not required.)

Instructions regarding War Diaries and Intelligence Summaries are contained in F. S. Regs., Part II. and the Staff Manual respectively. Title pages will be prepared in manuscript.

Place	Date	Hour	Summary of Events and Information	Remarks and references to Appendices
ROUSSEL FARM	15/8		Attended duties of section. Worked units made improvements to Camp.	Apx
"	16/8		Attended duties of section. Worked units improvements to Camp. Inoculated men known colongen. 1 XI Corps V.E.S.	Apx
	17/8		Attended duties of section, worked units made improvements to Camp.	Apx
			Inoculated 2.10 men belonging to 6th Division. 1 XI Corps V.E.S. 2nd on scheme	
	18/8		Attended duties of section. Worked units made improvements to Camp	Apx
	19/8		Attended duties of section. Worked units made improvements to Camp Evacuated 10 men & 2 Mules (9 horses & 1 mule belonging) 1 E/1st du	Apx
	20/8		Attended duties of section. Worked units made improvements to Camp	Apx
			Attended conference of DADVS.	
	21/8		Attended duties of section. Worked units made	Apx
	22/8		Attended duties of section. worked units made improvements to Camp.	Apx
			Evacuated 9 horses & 1 mule sick 6.1st Division F XI Corps V.E.S.	
	23/8		Attended duties of section. Worked units made improvements to Camp	Apx
	24/8		Attended duties of section. worked units made improvements to Camp	Apx
			Evacuated 8 horses sick 61st Div. F XI Corps V.E.S.	
	25/8		Attended duties of section. Worked units made improvements to Camp	Apx
	26/8		Attended duties of section. Worked units made improvements to Camp	Apx
	27/8		Attended duties of section. Worked units made improvements to Camp	Apx
			Attended conference of D.A.V.S.	

Army Form C. 2118.

WAR DIARY
or
INTELLIGENCE SUMMARY.
(Erase heading not required.)

Instructions regarding War Diaries and Intelligence Summaries are contained in F. S. Regs., Part II. and the Staff Manual respectively. Title pages will be prepared in manuscript.

Place	Date	Hour	Summary of Events and Information	Remarks and references to Appendices
ROUSSEL FARM.	28.9.18		Attended duties of Section. Evacuated 7 Horses & 1 Mule, 5 Horses & 1 Mule belonging to 61st Division. Visited Units.	
"	29.9.18		Attended to duties of Section. Visited Units. Carried on with internment of Cattle.	
"	30.9.18		Attended to duties of Section. Visited Units. Handed over to Capt Blossom.	

G.M. Blossom
Capt A.V.C.

WAR DIARY
or
INTELLIGENCE SUMMARY.

(Erase heading not required.)

Army Form C. 2118

Instructions regarding War Diaries and Intelligence Summaries are contained in F. S. Regs., Part II. and the Staff Manual respectively. Title pages will be prepared in manuscript.

Place	Date	Hour	Summary of Events and Information	Remarks and references to Appendices
ROUSSEL FARM	1/10/18		Evacuated 2 Horses, 1 belonging to 61st Division, other of Section	G.R.B.
"	2/10/18		Visited Units & inspected Cooks, Messrooms.	G.R.B.
"	3/10/18		Evacuated 6 Horses & 1 Mule & 1 Horse & 1 Mule belonging to 61st Division attached other Units	G.R.B.
"			1 Mules Corporal D.A.D.V.S. looked up preparation for moving. Evacuated 5 Horses & 1 Mule & 1 Horse & 1 Mule belonging to 61st Division	G.R.B. G.R.B.
LAMBRES	4/10/18		Mons Section GLAMBRES attached to Details. Settled in & cleared up Billets.	G.R.B.
"	5/10/18		Evacuated 3 Horses belonging to 61st Division. Visited Units attached to the Section	G.R.B.
GEZAINCOURT	6/10/18		Moved Section by train to GEZAINCOURT.	G.R.B.
"	7/10/18		Visited Units attached Section of Section	G.R.B. G.R.B.
BRETONCOURT	8/10/18		Moved Section to BRETONCOURT.	G.R.B.
ST LEGER	9/10/18		Moved Section to ST LEGER.	G.R.B.
MORCHIES	10/10/18		Moved Section to MORCHIES.	G.R.B.
GRAINCOURT	11/10/18		Evacuated 1 Horse belonging 61st Division to XVII Corps V.E.S. Moved Section to GRAINCOURT	G.R.B.
			Area E.28.a.6.4. & took over from 59. H.M. + 5 & 9 Horses & 1 Mule.	

Army Form C. 2118.

WAR DIARY
or
INTELLIGENCE SUMMARY.
(Erase heading not required.)

Instructions regarding War Diaries and Intelligence Summaries are contained in F.S. Regs. Part II. and the Staff Manual respectively. Title pages will be prepared in manuscript.

Place	Date	Hour	Summary of Events and Information	Remarks and references to Appendices
GRAINCOURT	12/10/18		Found and visited Units, attached duties of Section, cleaned up and lines	G.W.B.
"	13/10/18		Destroyed & burned 1 horse belonging 7th Royal Fusiliers 63 R.N. Division	G.W.B.
"	14/10/18		Evacuated 1 in Horses +3 Mules, 7 Horses +2 Mules belonging to 61st Division	G.W.B.
"	15/10/18		Attends duties of Section & visited Units.	G.W.B.
"	16/10/18		Evacuated 8 Horses to 17 V.E.S., 1 Animal belonging to 61st Division visited Units + attended other duties	G.W.B.
"	17/10/18		Attends duties of Section & visited Units.	G.W.B.
"	18/10/18		Attends duties of Section, attended Conference of D.D.V.S. visited Units.	G.W.B.
			Moved Section to 1 Rue St Quentin, CAMBRAI, Collected Stray H-D, Channel out and inspect Billets. Issued Stray Rider to 307 R.F.A.	G.W.B.
CAMBRAI	18/10/18		Moved Section to RIEUX. Evacuated 2 Horses to XVII V.E.S., 1 horse belonging 61st Division, cleaned Billets re, tallments other duties of Section	
RIEUX	19/10/18		Attends duties of Section & Units, proceeded with cleaning of Billets + 200 for ? state.	G.W.B.
"	20/10/18		Evacuated 1 horse & XVII V.E.S. other than 61st Division visited Units + attends other duties of Section	G.W.B.
"	21/10/18		Evacuated 1 horse & XVII V.E.S., 1 horse belonging to 61st Division, visited Units & videpradis.	G.W.B.
"	22/10/18		Evacuated 11 Horses + 1 Mule to XVII V.E.S., D.A.D.V.S. 19th Division retaking over.	G.W.B.

Army Form C. 2118.

WAR DIARY
or
INTELLIGENCE SUMMARY.
(Erase heading not required.)

61 M.V.S.   Vol 3

Place	Date	Hour	Summary of Events and Information	Remarks and references to Appendices
AVESNES-LEZ-AUBERT	23/10/18		Moved Section to AVESNES-LEZ-AUBERT, went forward with billetting party, found billets, moved in, cleaned billets, visited units.	G.M.B.
"	24/10/18		Evacuated 4 Horses & 2 Mules to XVII V.E.S. 1 Horse belonging to 61st Division, visited French Mission & arranged shoe butchery for Oxteam, slaughtered one horse. Visited billets, purchased kit cleaning billets.	G.M.B.
"	25/10/18		Evacuated 13 Horses & 2 Mules to XVII V.E.S. 3 Horses & 1 Mule belonging to 61st Division. Visited units, visited ST. AUBERT re billetting, attended other duties of Section.	G.M.B.
MAISON-BLEU	26/10/19		Moved Section to MAISON-BLEU & attended to duties of Section. Evacuated 5 Horses after Max 64th Division to XVII V.E.S.	G.M.B.
"	27/10/		Proceeded with cleaning of Billets, etc. day, attended to duties of Section	G.M.B.
"	28/10/18		Visited Units. Ordered improvement of Billets, & attended duties of Section	G.M.B.
"	29/10/18		Visited Units & attended duties of Section	G.M.B.
"	30/10/18		Evacuated 11 Horses & 3 Mules to XVII V.E.S. 9 Horses & 2 Mules belonging to 61st Division. Visited Units.	G.M.B
"	31/10/18		Evacuated 26 Horses to XVII V.E.S. 19 Horses belonging to 61st Division. Visited Units & attended to other duties of Section.	G.M.B

G.M. Blossome Capt. A.V.C.

Army Form C. 2118.

61 Div
Stat Vet [illegible]
Vet 32

WAR DIARY
or
INTELLIGENCE SUMMARY.

(Erase heading not required.)

Instructions regarding War Diaries and Intelligence Summaries are contained in F. S. Regs., Part II. and the Staff Manual respectively. Title pages will be prepared in manuscript.

Place	Date	Hour	Summary of Events and Information	Remarks and references to Appendices
MAISON-BLEU	1/11/18		Visited Units & attended to duties of Section & improvement of Billets.	G.W.B.
"	2/11/18		Attended to duties of Section, arranged with O.C. 2nd Div. M.B.S. re fitting O.R.H. prepared to move. Visited Units.	G.W.B.
AVESNES-LEZ-AUBERT	3/11/18		Moved Section to AVESNES-LEZ-AUBERT, visited Units; attended to the duties of Section	G.W.B.
"	4/11/18		Evacuated 11 Horses & 2 Mules to XVII V.E.S. 5 Horses & 1 Mule belonging to 61st Division. Cleaned up Billets & Visited Units.	G.W.B.
"	5/11/18		Evacuated 3 Horses & 1 Mule to XVII V.E.S., 2 Horses & 1 Mule belonging to 61st Division. Issued 7 New Horses to Cast. Posts	G.W.B. F.W.B
"	6/11/18		Attended to duties of Section, cleaned up Billets, movement orders	G.W.B.
"	7/11/18		Attended conferences D.A.D.V.S., attended duties of Section, prepared to move.	G.W.B.
BERMERAIN	8/11/18		Moved Section to BERMERAIN, visited Units, Evacuated 1 Horse to XVII V.E.S. belonging to 61st Division	G.W.B.
"	9/11/18		Attended to duties of Section, cleaned up Billets.	G.W.B.
"	10/11/18		Attended duties of Section, inspect Billets & visited Units.	G.W.B
"	11/11/18		Attended duties of Section, visited Units & cleaned Billets. Armistice terms ceased at 11 O'Clock.	G.W.B

Army Form C. 2118.

WAR DIARY
or
INTELLIGENCE SUMMARY.

(Erase heading not required.)

Instructions regarding War Diaries and Intelligence Summaries are contained in F. S. Regs., Part II. and the Staff Manual respectively. Title pages will be prepared in manuscript.

Place	Date	Hour	Summary of Events and Information	Remarks and references to Appendices
BERMERAIN	12/2/18		Attended duties of Section, visited Units.	G.M.B.
"	13/2/18		Attended duties of Section, visited Units. Cleaned Billets, with one section of D.A.D.V.S.	G.M.B.
RIEUX	14/2/18		Moved Section to RIEUX. Evacuated 3 Horses x 1 Mule to XVII V.E.S. all attended.	G.M.B.
			belonging to 61st Division, attended duties of Section & D.A.D.S	G.M.B.
CAMBRAI	15/2/18		Moved Section to CAMBRAI, Cleaned out Billets, attended duties of Section & D.A.D.V.S.	G.M.B.
"	16/2/18		Visited Units, inspected Billets, attended other duties of Section & D.A.D.V.S.	G.M.B.
"	17/2/18		Visited Units, attended duties of Section & D.A.D.V.S.	G.M.B.
"	18/2/18		Visited Units, attended duties of Section & D.A.D.V.S.	G.M.B.
"	19/2/18		Visited Units, attended duties of Section & D.A.D.V.S.	G.M.B.
"	20/2/18		Attended to duties of Section & D.A.D.V.S.	G.M.B.
"	21/2/18		Visited Units, attended to duties of Section & D.A.D.V.S.	G.M.B.
"	22/2/18		Visited Units, attended to duties of Section & D.A.D.V.S. Evacuated 9 Horses & 2 Mules to XVII V.E.S at SOLESMES. 4 Horses & 2 Mules belonging to 61st Division.	G.M.B.
"	23/2/18		Attended to duties of Section & D.A.D.V.S.	G.M.B.
BEUGNATRE	24/2/16		Moved Section to BEUGNATRE	G.M.B.

D. D. & L., London, E.C.
(A804) Wt. W1271/M2 31 750,000 5/17 **Sch. 52** Forms/C2118/14

Army Form C. 2118.

WAR DIARY
or
INTELLIGENCE SUMMARY.
(Erase heading not required)

Instructions regarding War Diaries and Intelligence Summaries are contained in F.S. Regs., Part II. and the Staff Manual respectively. Title pages will be prepared in manuscript.

Place	Date	Hour	Summary of Events and Information	Remarks and references to Appendices
ST LEGER.	25/8		Moved Section to ST LEGER.	G.M.B.
VACQUERIE	26/8		Moved Section to VACQUERIE	G.M.B.
"	27/8		Cleaned at Bihel + attended duties of Section rDADVS.	G.M.B.
"	28/8		Visited Units rattending duties of Section rDADVS.	G.M.B.
"	29/8		Visited Units rattending duties of Section rDADVS.	G.M.B.
"	30/8		Attended duties of Section. Certain details, orders, of DADVS.	G.M.B.

G.M. Blaorne
Capt A.V.C.

WAR DIARY or INTELLIGENCE SUMMARY

Army Form C. 2118.

61 SM Vety Sec

Vol 33

Place	Date	Hour	Summary of Events and Information	Remarks and references to Appendices
VACQUERIE	1/12/18		Attended to duties of Section, visited Units & attended duties of D.A.D.V.S.	G.W.B.
"	2/12/18		Evacuated 11 Horses & 1 Mule to XVII V.E.S. DOULLENS. 1 Horse & 1 Mule (all belonging to 61st Div) attended duties of D.A.D.V.S.	G.W.B.
"	3/12/18		Attended to duties of Section, visited Unit, & attended duties of D.A.D.V.S.	G.W.B.
"	4/12/18		Evacuated 12 Horses & 1 Mule to XVII V.E.S. DOULLENS, all belonging to 61st Division	G.W.B.
"	5/12/18		Attended duties of D.A.D.V.S. & visited Unit. Attended duties of Section & visited Unit, attended duties of D.A.D.V.S.	G.W.B.
"	6/12/18		Evacuated 9 Horses & 1 Mule to XVII Corps & E.S. DOULLENS, attended to duties of Section (all belonging to 61st Division).	G.W.B.
"	7/12/18		Journey ONEUX & billeted Section, visited Col R.F.A. Marise, attended to the duties of Section & attended duties of D.A.D.V.S.	G.W.B.
ONEUX	8/12/18		Moved Section to ONEUX, cleaned out Billet & settled in, attended duties of D.A.D.V.S.	G.W.B.
"	9/12/18		Visited Units, proceeded with cleaning out of Billets & attended duties of Orderlies. Attended duties of D.A.D.V.S. to Major Innes.	G.W.B.
"	10/12/18		Visited Units & attended duties of Section. Evacuated 27 Horses & 1 Mule to XVII Mule & Horse Vet Hosp. ABBEVILLE, 2 Horses Alinguig to 61st Division	G.W.B.

WAR DIARY
or
INTELLIGENCE SUMMARY. 61st (S.M.) M. V.S.

Army Form C. 2118.

Place	Date	Hour	Summary of Events and Information	Remarks and references to Appendices
ONEUX	11/2/18		Visited Units, showed up Billets & attended to duties of Section	G.W.B.
"	12/2/18		Attended Conference D.A.D.V.S. attended duties of Section & visited Units	G.W.B.
"	13/2/18		Attended to duties of Section, visited Units, carried on with inspection of Billets.	G.W.B.
"	14/2/18		Evacuated 6 Horses to Mow Vet Hosp ABBEVILLE other than 61st Division visited Units, Bivouacs	G.W.B.
"	15/2/18		With meeting of receiving furniture for Billets	G.W.B.
"	16/2/18		Attended to duties of Section, visited Units	G.W.B.
"			Evacuated 8 Horses to Mow Vet Hosp ABBEVILLE, also belonging to 6th Division visited Units	G.W.B.
"			Met moving furniture for men hereabouts, & otherwise attended to Duties of Section	G.W.B.
"			Erected Pharmacy, visited Units, attended to Duties of Section, supplies made	G.W.B.
"	17/2/18		Ira ora for Corthause; Visited Units, attended duties of Section, proceeded with Inspection of Billets, conducted	G.W.B.
"	18/2/18		Evacuated 41 Horses & 7 Mules to 14 Vet Hosp. ABBEVILLE. (Horses) & Mal Intergers to 61st Division, repeated Shells & attended duties of Section, attended Conference S.A.D.V.S.	G.W.B.
"	19/2/18		Unions duties of Section, repeated Shells, seen tracts beds for Section	G.W.B.
"	20/2/18		Attended duties of Section, visited Units & inspected Billets & inspected	G.W.B.
"	21/2/18 22/2/18		Visited Attended Duties of Section, visited Billets, followed duties of Section	G.W.B.

61

Army Form C. 2118.

WAR DIARY
or
INTELLIGENCE SUMMARY.
(Erase heading not required.)

61st C.M.J.M.V.S.

Vol 34

Place	Date	Hour	Summary of Events and Information	Remarks and references to Appendices
ONEUX	1/19		Attended to duties of Section. Veterinary Board visited units	G.W.B.
"	2/19		Evacuated 15 horses & mules with 1st Mob A.V. Hosp. ABBEVILLE. 15 horses & 5 mules belonging to 61st Division, attached to duties of Section	G.W.B.
"	3/19		Attended to duties of Section. Supervised & billets & duties of Veterinary Board	G.W.B.
"	4/19		Evacuated 14 horses to 14 Vet Hosp. ABBEVILLE. 5 horses belonging to 61st Division. Attended to duties of Section & Veterinary Board. Visiting units	G.W.B.
"	5/19		Attended to duties of Section. Conducted Bath for men	G.W.B.
"	6/19		Evacuated 5 horses & 1 mule to Mob Vet Hosp ABBEVILLE. Completed Bath-house for men & carried out duties of Veterinary Board. Beard all animals evacuated belonging to 61st Division. Attended to the duties of Section	G.W.B.
"	7/19		Attended to duties of Veterinary Board. Board & duties of Section	G.W.B.
"	8/19		Evacuated 5 horses & 4 mules all belonging to 61st Division. Attended to duties of Section + Veterinary Board. Visited units	G.W.B.
"	9/19		Duties of Section & carried on with Vet Board. Board. Visited units	G.W.B.
"	10/19		Attended to duties of Section + Veterinary Board. Board. Attended to duties of Section + Veterinary Board. 6 horses 6 61st Division.	G.W.B.
"	11/19		Attended to duties of Section + Veterinary Board. 2 mules 13 horses belonging to 61st Division. All attached to duties of Section + Veterinary Board.	G.W.B.

WAR DIARY
or
INTELLIGENCE SUMMARY.
(Erase heading not required.)

Army Form C. 2118.

61 VSM/MVS

Place	Date	Hour	Summary of Events and Information	Remarks and references to Appendices
ONEUX	1/19		Attended to duties of section, Veterinary Board visited units	G.M.B
"	2/19		Evacuated 15 horses & mules 61st Vet Hosp ABBEVILLE, 15 horses & mules bringing to 61st Division, attended to duties of section	G.M.B
"	3/19		Attended to duties of section, in pursuance of Bittets & duties of Veterinary Board	G.M.B
"	4/19		Evacuated 14 horses to the 1st Aux. ABBEVILLE, 5 horses belonging to 61st Division handed duties of section, Veterinary Board visiting units	G.M.B
"	5/19		Attended to duties of section, Constructed Bath for men.	G.M.B
"	6/19		Evacuated 8 horses & 1 mule to 1st Aux. Vet Hosp. ABBEVILLE, Completed Bath house for men & carried on with duties of Veterinary Board. Board all animals & vehicles belong to 61st Division, attended also duties of section.	G.M.B
"	7/19		Attended duties of Veterinary Board, Board + duties of section	G.M.B
"	8/19		Evacuated 8 horses & 4 mules all belonging to 61st Division, attended to duties of section + carried on with Vet. Board, Board visited units.	G.M.B
"	9/19		Duties of section + carried on with Vet. Church Board. Board.	G.M.B
"	10/19		Attended to duties of section + Veterinary Board.	G.M.B
"	11/19		Attended to duties of section + Veterinary Board, 13 horses belonging to 61st Division, attended to duties of section, Veterinary Board.	G.M.B

Army Form C. 2118.

WAR DIARY
or
INTELLIGENCE SUMMARY. 6th (I.M.) M.V.S.
(Erase heading not required.)

Instructions regarding War Diaries and Intelligence Summaries are contained in F. S. Regs., Part II. and the Staff Manual respectively. Title pages will be prepared in manuscript.

Place	Date	Hour	Summary of Events and Information	Remarks and references to Appendices
ONEUX	12/2/19		Evacuated 12 Horses & 2 Mules, 2 Horses belonging to 6th Division. Carried on with duties of Pct. Disinf. Board taking duties of Section	G.M.B.
"	13/2/19		Attended duties of Section. Carried on with duties of Pct. Disinf. Board.	G.M.B.
"	14/2/19		Attended duties of Section. Carried on with duties of Pct. Disinf. Board.	G.M.B.
"	15/2/19		Attended duties of Section. Carried on with duties of Pct. Disinf. Board.	G.M.B
"	16/2/19		Attended Conference D.A.D.V.S. & duties of Section. Carried on with duties of Pct. Disinf. Board.	G.M.B.
"	17/2/19		Attended duties of Section. Carried on with duties of Pct. Disinf. Board. Evacuated 3 Horses all belonging to 6th Division.	G.M.B
"	18/2/19		Attended duties of Section. Carried on with duties of 1st Divnl. Board. Despatches (1/2/3) sent but pistol.	G.M.B.
"	19/2/19		Attended duties of Section & visited Units.	G.M.B.
"	20/2/19		Attended duties of Section & visited Units.	G.M.B.
"	21/2/19		Attended duties of Section & Disinf. Pct. Board.	G.M.B
"	22/2/19		Attended duties of Section & Veterinary Disinf. Board, visited Units.	G.M.B.

WAR DIARY
or
INTELLIGENCE SUMMARY. 61st (S.M.) M.V.S.

Army Form C. 2118.

Place	Date	Hour	Summary of Events and Information	Remarks and references to Appendices
ONEUX.	23/9		Evacuated 3 Horses & 6 Mules to 31st Vet. Hosp. ABBEVILLE. 2 Horses & 5 Mules belonging to 61st Division attached Convoys.	G.W.B.
"	24/9		Attended duties of Section. DADVS took duties of Section.	G.W.B.
"	25/9		Attended duties of Section. Mallein tested 4 2 Y's Z at 2/8 Worcesters Regt. Evacuated 1 Horse (Curb) belonging 61st Division to 31st Vet Hosp ABBEVILLE.	G.W.B.
"	26/9		Attended duties of Section & visited Units.	G.W.B.
"	27/9		Attended duties of Section.	G.W.B.
"	28/9		Attended duties of Section & visited Units.	G.W.B.
"	29/9		Attended duties of Section & visited Units.	G.W.B.
"	30/9		Attended duties of Section. Evacuated 4 Horses & 4 Mules + 2 Mules belonging 61st Division, visited Units, / now Evacuated Hospital Influenza.	G.W.B.
"	31/9		Attended Convoys ADVS. DADVS attended duties of Section.	G.W.B.
"			6 Men Evacuated Hospital Influenza, attended duties of Section.	G.W.B.

J.H. Bloom Capt. R.A.V.C.

WAR DIARY or INTELLIGENCE SUMMARY

Army Form C. 2118.

61st (S.M.) M.T.S. Vol 35

Instructions regarding War Diaries and Intelligence Summaries are contained in F.S. Regs., Part II. and the Staff Manual respectively. Title pages will be prepared in manuscript.

Place	Date	Hour	Summary of Events and Information	Remarks and references to Appendices
ONEUX	1/1/19		Attended duties of Section. Evacuated 3 men to Hospital Influenza. Left with total personnel of 6 O.R.	G.W.B.
"	2/1/19		One driver A.S.C. arrived. Mallam sick. 6 O.R. M.G.B. M.	G.W.B.
"	3/1/19		Sam with Influenza. Carried on as well as possible.	G.W.B.
"	4/1/19		Attended to duties of Section	G.W.B.
"	5/1/19		Attended to duties of Section	G.W.B.
"	6/1/19		Attended to duties of Section. Cpl Harrison evacuated to hospital P.U.O.	G.W.B.
"	7/1/19		Attended to duties of Section	G.W.B.
"	8/1/19		Attended to duties of Section. Pte Stanton returned off leave. Attd Rodgers transferred from hospital to R.A.M.C. from 182 Inf Bde reports for duty	G.W.B.
"	9/1/19		Attended to duties of Section. Sergt gave P.A.S.C. from 182 Inf Bde reports for duty. Pte Johns returned from hospital	G.W.B.
"	10/1/19		Evacuated 4 Horses 1 Mule to horse hospital. 2 Horses 1 Mule belonging to 61st Division attached to duties of Section	G.W.B.
"	11/1/19		Attended to duties of Section	G.W.B.

Army Form C. 2118.

WAR DIARY
or
INTELLIGENCE SUMMARY.
(Erase heading not required.)

6th (S.M.) Bat. H.L.Ies.

Instructions regarding War Diaries and Intelligence Summaries are contained in F. S. Regs., Part II. and the Staff Manual respectively. Title pages will be prepared in manuscript.

Place	Date	Hour	Summary of Events and Information	Remarks and references to Appendices
ONEUX	12/2/19		Evacuated 2 Horses to No 14 Vet Hosp. Also belonging to 61st Division also Evacuated 3 Spare Mules to No 2 Advanced Remount Depot also 2 other Mules of Section	G.W.B.
"	13/2/19		Attends to duties of Section	G.W.B.
"	14/19		Evacuated 3 Horses & 2 Mules to No 14 Vet Hosp. 2 Mules & 1 Horse belonging to 61st Division	G.W.B.
"	"		Attends to the duties of Section	G.W.B.
"	15/2/19		Attends to duties of Section	G.W.B.
"	16/2/19		Attends to duties of Section. Pte Ing admitted to S.J. 2 A.F. Lumbago.	G.W.B.
"	17/19		Evacuated 2 Horses & 1 Mule to No 14 V.H. 1 Horse & 1 Mule belonging to 61st Division. Attends to duties of Section	G.W.B.
"	18/2/19		Attends to duties of Section	G.W.B.
"	19/2/19		Attends to duties of Section. Pte McDougall admitted 3/1 S.A. Scabies feet.	G.W.B.
"	20/19		Attends to duties of Section	G.W.B.
"	21/2/19		Attends to duties of Section	G.W.B.
"	22/19		Attends to duties of Section	G.W.B.
"	23/2/19		Attends to duties of Section	G.W.B.
"	24/19		Attends to duties of Section Evacuated 4 Mules & 2 Horses to No 14 V.H. 3 Mules & 2 Horses belonging to 61st Division	G.W.B.

Army Form C. 2118.

WAR DIARY
or
INTELLIGENCE SUMMARY. 61ᵒʳ (S.M.) M.A.S.

(Erase heading not required.)

Instructions regarding War Diaries and Intelligence Summaries are contained in F. S. Regs., Part II. and the Staff Manual respectively. Title pages will be prepared in manuscript.

Place	Date	Hour	Summary of Events and Information	Remarks and references to Appendices
ONEUX	25/10		Attended to duties of Section	G.W.B. Sch. B
"	26/10		Attended to duties of Section, 2 Sergts, 2 Cpls & 5 Smith evacuated sick	Sch. B
"	27/10		Attended to duties of Section, 2 Mule Transport drivers reported for duty from No 1. Co Bn Div Train.	G.W.B
"	28/10		Evacuated 4 Horses & 2 Mules to 14 Vet Hospital. 1 Horse & 1 Mule belonging to 61st Division. Attacks attended to Tunnels since at 23.00, attended other duties of Section	G.W.B.

G.W. Brown
Capt R.A.V.C.

WAR DIARY
or
INTELLIGENCE SUMMARY.
(Erase heading not required.)

Army Form C. 2118.

61st D.V.S.

Vol 36

Place	Date	Hour	Summary of Events and Information	Remarks and references to Appendices
ON FLIX	1/3/19		Attended to duties of Section	G.W.B.
"	2/3/19		Attended to duties of Section & Civilian Cases.	G.W.B.
"	3/3/19		Attended to duties of Section	G.W.B.
"	4/3/19		Evacuated 3 Horses to No 14 Vet. Hosp. all belonging to 61st Division. 2 Mules otc.	
"	5/3/19		Duties of Section & Civilian Cases.	G.W.B.
"			Attended duties of Section	G.W.B.
"	6/3/19		Attended Conference of O.s.C. D.V.S. & other duties of Section	G.W.B.
"	7/3/19		Evacuated 5 Horses 24 Mules to No 14 Vet Hosp. 2 Horses belonging to 61st Division & attended other duties of Section	G.W.B.
"	8/3/19		Attended duties of Section & Civilian Cases.	G.W.B.
"	9/3/19		Attended duties of Section	G.W.B.
"	10/3/19		Lt. McDougal returned duty from S.I.D.H. Evacuated 4 Mules, 2 Mules belong to 61st Division, attended other duties of Section & civilian cases.	G.W.B.
"	11/3/19		Attended duties of Section visited O/C Lane Cases declined orders for sick civils.	G.W.B.
"	12/3/19		Sent Lt. Capetin of Jeep's, applied for Independent return 3 Mules duties of Section & visited Civilian Cases.	G.W.B.

Army Form C. 2118.

WAR DIARY
or
INTELLIGENCE SUMMARY.

(Erase heading not required.)

Eper (S.M.) Mob. Vet. Sec.

Instructions regarding War Diaries and Intelligence Summaries are contained in F. S. Regs., Part II. and the Staff Manual respectively. Title pages will be prepared in manuscript.

Place	Date	Hour	Summary of Events and Information	Remarks and references to Appendices
DICKEBUSCH	13/7/19		Evacuated 2 Horses & 1 Mule to Norm Vet Hospital. 3 Horses & 1 Mule belonging to 61st Division attached strength of Section (Civilian Cases).	G.W.B.
"	14/7/19		Evacuated 9 Horses to No 14 Vet Hospital, all belonging to 61st Division.	G.W.B.
"	15/7/19		Attend to duties of Section. Pte Butcher demobilised, & proceeds to Concentration Camp Alberille.	G.W.B.
"	16/7/19		Attend to duties of Section (Civilian Cases).	G.W.B.
"	17/7/19		Attend to duties of Section (Civilian Cases).	G.W.B.
"	18/7/19		Handed over Section to Capt Proctor, R.A.V.C & proceed to England on Demobilisation.	G.W.B.

G.W.Blaker
Capt R.A.V.C.

Army Form C. 2118.

WAR DIARY
or
INTELLIGENCE SUMMARY.
(Erase heading not required.)

Instructions regarding War Diaries and Intelligence Summaries are contained in F. S. Regs., Part II. and the Staff Manual respectively. Title pages will be prepared in manuscript.

Place	Date	Hour	Summary of Events and Information	Remarks and references to Appendices
ONE OX	18/3/19		Took command of Section from Capt S W Alexander who proceeded to England on demobilization	N.E
"	19/3/19		Pte W Shepperd of reinforcement draft of taken for duty. Attached duties of section & various cases	N.E
"	20/3/19		Evacuated 3 hours to Mil 14 Vilenary hospital all 61st Div	N.E
"	21/3/19		Attended duties of section & various cases & remits 7 61st Div. Evacuated 3 hours to Mil 14 V.H. hospital all 61st Div.	N.E
"	22/3/19		Attended duties of section & various cases & remits of 61st Div. Attended duties of section and units of 61st Div.	N.E
"	23/3/19		Attended duties of section and units of 61st Div.	N.E
"	24/3/19		Evacuated 2 horses & 2 mules to 14 Vet Hospital (61st Div) Att. duties of section & various units of 61st Div	N.E
"	25/3/19		Att. duties of section & various units of 61st Div	N.E
"	26/3/19		Evac. duties of section & various units of 61st Div Evac 1 horse to 14 Vet hospital	N.E
"	27/3/19		Cpl Gumley J, Pte Anthony RM & Pte Vann I demobilized & proceeded to evacuation camp Etaples Attended duties of section & units of 61st Div	N.E
"	28/3/19		Attended duties of section & units of 61st Div	N.E
"	29/3/19		Evacuated six horses to 14 Vet Hospital & 2 horses of section	N.E
"	30/3/19		Attended duties of section & units of 61st Div	N.E
"	31/3/19		Attended duties of section & units of 61st Div	N.E

M J Wells Capt RAVC